Inspire, Enlighten, & Motivate

This book is dedicated to those who
Inspired, Enlightened, & Motivated me.
They are too many to name—
Too important to forget.

Inspire, Enlighten, & Motivate

Great Thoughts to Enrich Your Next Speech and You

Noah benShea

CORWIN PRESS, INC.
A Sage Publications Company
Thousand Oaks, California

For information:

Corwin Press, Inc.
A Sage Publications Company
2455 Teller Road
Thousand Oaks, California 91320
www.corwinpress.com

Sage Publications Ltd.
6 Bonhill Street
London EC2A 4PU
United Kingdom

Sage Publications India Pvt. Ltd.
B-42 Panchsheel Enclave
New Delhi 110 017 India

Printed in the United States of America

Library of Congress Cataloging-in-Publication Data

benShea, Noah.
Inspire, enlighten, & motivate: Great thoughts to enrich your next speech and you / Noah benShea.
       p. cm.
ISBN 0-7619-3866-4 (acid-free paper) — ISBN 0-7619-3867-2 (pbk. : acid-free paper)
     1. Public speaking. 2. Conduct of life—Anecdotes. 3. Exempla.
I. Title: Inspire, enlighten, and motivate. II. Title.
PN4193.I5B38 2003
808.5´1—dc21

                                        2002154781

This book is printed on acid-free paper.

03   04   05   06   10   9   8   7   6   5   4   3   2   1

Acquisitions Editor:	Robert D. Clouse
Associate Editor:	Kristen L. Gibson
Editorial Assistant:	Erin Clow
Production Editor:	Diane S. Foster
Copy Editor:	Kristen Bergstad
Typesetter:	C&M Digitals (P) Ltd.
Proofreader:	Taryn Bigelow
Cover Designer:	Tracy E. Miller
Production Artist:	Janet Foulger

Contents

Preface

I have spent a lifetime learning and learning how to communicate. And I'd like to share some of that learning with you. I do this not because I know so much but because what you know is so important, and because it's important that what you know be listened to and heard.

Inevitably in the life of an educator you will be called on to give a speech. You may be called on to exult, exalt, or mourn. You may be called on to be persuasive, passionate, or politic. You may be called upon to address students, parents, a panel, or even a mob. Your time may be limited, expansive, or interrupted, and sometimes all three. However and whenever you are called upon, the format and audience are going to vary.

What this book will provide are ideas, and stories, and one-liners, and point makers, and points of reflection designed to spur and serve your thinking, lend you inspiration, offer you perhaps a compass on a path of thinking less commonly traveled. This book is indexed for easy access and cross-referencing to ideas, and, with this book as with so many things in life, where you begin is not important, but simply beginning is.

In the film industry, an outside writer is often called in just before filming to "punch up" a script. This is a book geared to give your presentation more punch. This is a book of speech starters, and finishers, and ways of looking at things that will have others listening to you and nodding their heads.

Too often educators feel that they are shouting in the wind. Here are ways to whisper with the wind and be heard across generations. You are the leader, the educator, the star that others look to. Following are thoughts, reflections, and ideas that need your words to surround them, to frame them, and to support them so they can best support you when circumstances require you to speak to an audience, or when you are simply introduced and asked to say a few words. So whether you're asked to congratulate, motivate, persuade, justify, or even express concern, here is an ally in your effort.

Kind critics have long said that because I write epigrammatically, my work serves the spoken word. Hopefully this approach will serve your presentations. Hopefully it will open a world, or a world of reflection, in a single line. The Gettysburg Address was written on the back of an envelope. Impromptu speeches always take the most time to write. Mark Twain said that what he liked about children is that they tell you what they have to say and then stop. And the famed educator John Dewey reminded all speakers that there is a world of difference between saying something and having something to say. This is not a book for the long-winded, but for those who would like their remarks long remembered.

This book is written not only to enrich your speeches, as the title suggests, but also to enrich you, the reader. Life is a lesson in process, and about process. It is an adventure in learning as heartwarming as it is heart wrenching. Herein are my field notes. What binds us one to another is not what we look at, but how we look at it. Enjoy the view!

Lastly, as my work is offered in support of any presentation, please be sure to cite the author. The author thanks you.

—Noah benShea
Santa Barbara, California

About the Author

 **Noah benShea** is a poet, philosopher, scholar, humorist, lecturer, and international best-selling author who was, by the age of 23, an Assistant Dean of Students at UCLA and by 30, a consulting fellow to the esteemed Center for the Study of Democratic Institutions in Santa Barbara, California. His first book, a collection of poetry titled *Don't Call It Anything,* received the Schull Award from the Southern California Poetry Society. He has lectured at numerous universities and has given a keynote address at the Library of Congress. His work has been included in publications of Oxford University and the World Bible Society in Jerusalem.

Often referred to as the guru's guru, Noah benShea is the author of 14 books, including the broadly loved *Jacob the Baker* series, which is translated around the world and embraced as timeless fables. His insightful perspective on life, *Noah's Window,* is carried globally via the Internet and was enjoyed by countless readers for many years via the *New York Times* Newspaper Regional Network. His essays were nominated for a Pulitzer Prize in Journalism in 1997, and in 1999 he was nominated for the Grawemeyer Award for Ideas Improving the World. His most recent book, *Remembering This My Children* is a collection of Mr. benShea's original thoughts twined with heart-touching photographs intended as a timeless legacy between parents and children and was chosen as a *Foreword Magazine* Finalist for Gift

Book of the Year. In addition to his reflective life, Mr. benShea was a founding partner and later chairman of a national manufacturing company, and he continues to serve as an advisor to North American business and community leaders. Born in Toronto, Canada, Mr. benShea has a daughter, Jordan, and a son, Adam, and lives in Santa Barbara, California.

Mr. benShea may be contacted at www.noahswindow.com or noah@noahswindow.com.

1

Welcome to School

We can't make moments. But we can make the most of them.

Never in the history of the planet have individuals with so much power felt so powerless. Never before have so many of us been told we are valued yet felt like vassals. Inside this personal-power-schizophrenia, that we matter often slips our minds because others appear to matter more. To that end here is a quiz I'd like you to take. I don't know if it will help you find your way, but it might remind and rearrange your thinking about how important you are along the way.

For the sake of conversation let's call this an Impact Quiz.

Here is the first of two parts:

1. Name the five wealthiest people in the world.

2. Name the last five Heisman Trophy winners.

3. Name the last five winners of the Miss America contest.

4. Name five people who have won a Nobel or Pulitzer Prize.

5. Name the last five Academy Award winners for best actor or actress.

How did you do? The point is, few, if any, of us remember the headliners of yesterday, and these are no second-rate achievers. These are the best in their fields. But the applause dies. Awards tarnish. Achievements are forgotten. Accolades and certificates are buried with their owners. Every stage eventually goes dark.

Here's the second half of the quiz. See how you do on this one:

1. List two teachers who aided your journey through school.

2. Name three friends who have helped you through a difficult time.

3. Name five people who have taught you something worthwhile.

4. Think of a few people who have made you feel appreciated and special.

5. Think of five people you enjoy spending time with.

Easier? The lesson?

The people who make a difference in our lives are not the ones with the most credentials, the most money, or the most awards. They are the ones who care. If you care, you make a difference.

⎯⎯⸱⸱⎯⎯

What makes our little corner of the world less isn't its size but our regard for it.

What diminishes us isn't only how others size us up but how we size ourselves up.

We begin to make ourselves more important by first refusing to diminish our importance.

Little adds more to our importance than knowing how important we are to each other.

We can't love others until we feel we can love ourselves, and love is a ladder that allows us to climb out of ourselves. Follow the path with a heart. At the heart of teaching is loving.

⎯⎯⸱⸱⎯⎯

The only equity we have in life is how we invest ourselves in the moment.

At any moment the question is where are we in that moment.

⎯⎯⸱⸱⎯⎯

We make the common profound by pausing and tying knots around a moment. In this way we transform our moments into a string of pearls.

⎯⎯⸱⸱⎯⎯

OVER EVERY FINISH LINE IN LIFE
ARE THE WORDS,
"BEGIN HERE"

All right. Here we are folks. Step up. Step up. Labor Day is done. Summer is over. School is in. The wheel that never stops turning has turned. Again. It's time to hunker down and get to work. Runners take your mark. There's a race to be run. What's never begun is never won.

On my internal calendar, September is January. And not just for me. Perhaps because so many of us spent so many years in school, or perhaps because so many of us spent so many years sending our kids off to school, September just feels like the starting gate. September is so pregnant with beginnings that in many ways it is more of a doorway to the year ahead than New Year's, the holiday that celebrates the Roman god of doors. And regardless of our ideas about where or when things ought to begin, very little begins at our beginning. Most begins where it begins.

Any of us who are planning to move forward can cut the cost on life's learning curve by taking the time to look backward.

Those who avoid the past never do.

Whether we're hoping, in the year ahead, to improve our chances of getting to heaven or simply to get better grades, all beginnings benefit from a backward glance.

The promises we make to ourselves about the future require us to look at promises we have broken in the past. Few of us who promise we'll study this year will honor that promise unless we study what or why we didn't do what we said we would do last year.

Getting better grades in any aspect of life requires us to take a hard look at what we didn't pass or passed on in the past.

Sooooo, sometimes the best way to approach new beginnings is by sitting down and quieting down before we go charging off.

While every beginning requires caution, we can also err on the side of caution. Beginnings require us, if you'll excuse the expression, to begin.

A buddy of mine in college would stay up for nights before finals creating elaborate study schedules. And never study. Plans can sometimes be a form of procrastination. It was the late John Lennon who reminded us: "Life is what happens while we're making plans."

Beginnings require preparation and reflection. But preparation and reflection are everything and nothing if nothing is done with them. Good deeds are prayer's wings.

If we want to begin to change the world, we have to begin with ourselves. "We don't see things as they are," wrote Anaïs Nin, "we see them as we are."

Most of us will do anything to begin anywhere but with ourselves. We will talk about changing our hair, our car, our neighborhood, or our job. But the real work begins here. At home. With us. Hello! Hello! Anyone home?

Beginning to work on one's self is just that. A beginning. Forget about finishing, even as we are reminded of the Talmudic teaching, "We are not expected to finish the work, but neither are we excused from it." Anyone who thinks they've finished their "work" is daydreaming and needs to get back to work. Unlike the movies, life is never a wrap. It is always a process. Outside of the individual ego, the camera in life never stops running. If or when the Great Director shouts "Cut," we'll all know it.

People used to live in one house most of their lives. And often worked for one company most of their lives. These were the standards of consistency that once reflected stability. Stability, however, has been redefined. Stability, we now realize, is a dynamic state. And, therein, its strength.

In early twentieth-century psychology it used to be that if your patient was drowning, you threw him a psychic rope and pulled the troubled soul to shore. By the 1950s it was generally observed that the shore of normalcy that a therapist stood on was illusionary and retreating. The shore it turns out is also dynamic.

Neither the patient nor the therapist was any longer sure where the shore was. What was once stability is now an aberration, at least statistically. It is only the variant family that now lives in the same house their whole life, and lots of movement in a business career often means you're a guy or gal on the move. Up. For many of us beginning new jobs or beginning life in a new home is what we're beginning to get used to. New beginnings are beginning to be old hat. And, like Dr. Seuss's character Bartholomew, some of us are wearing 500 of them.

Neurologists have long told us that anatomically the human brain resists change. Our mind likes to sort information and experiences down the same canals the information was sorted in the past. So, beginnings do challenge us. Beginnings challenge us to bend when we feel we just got something straight. But what beginnings beg us to see is that little is ending that isn't beginning. What does not bend, breaks.

Change is the only constant. Serial beginnings reflect the general state of change we live in.

Though this has always been true, these days it's not only visible, it's blinding. As change has accelerated, we are forced to adapt. Faster. Beginning to change is not something we can begin tomorrow. Beginning today, tomorrow will be yesterday.

———

A friend of mine named Lawrence Grobel has written a wonderful book titled *Talking With Michener*. This rich and fascinating insight into the life of James Michener reminded me of a story that Michener wrote of his childhood. About beginnings. And beginning again.

It seems that one fall day, when the famous author was a boy growing up in Pennsylvania, he found himself walking down a country road and happened on a fabulous apple tree laden with fruit. Coming closer he saw a farmer standing next to the tree. Seeing the boy admiring the tree, the farmer said, "Let me tell you about this tree. This is a very old tree and several years ago it stopped bearing fruit."

"What did you do?" asked Michener.

"Well," said the farmer, "I took a nail about a foot long and drove it into the tree's trunk. Next year it started bearing all over again. In fact, better than ever."

Every now and then, whether we want it, or like it, or seek it, something comes along that penetrates us so profoundly that we come alive all over again. Sometimes what shocks us revives us. Sometimes others or life nails us. Sometimes we have to nail ourselves.

It is true that all beginnings don't bear fruit, but every first step is a seed, planted. And in seeds there are orchards.

Time is also an orchard. Every moment is ripe with opportunity.

My grandfather, Jacob, used to say, "A man learns and learns and dies a fool." We all have a lot of learning to do. Fortunately, school is open.

2

Graduation and Matriculation

To borrow from Aldous Huxley, "Experience is not what happens to you; it is what you do with what happens to you."

Change is inevitable; progress is not.

Put more progress in your change.

WE'RE ALL IN GRADUATE SCHOOL

Linus Pauling won two Nobel Prizes: one in chemistry and one for peace. His prize in chemistry was for his insight on how molecular bodies bonded. He began thinking about the idea some years earlier, and then "one day while I was crossing a bridge, it came to me," said Pauling.

Insight arrives in its own good time. Every idea is a bridge from what we don't know to what we might yet learn. Or learn that we know. Most of us find ourselves crossing the bridge to learning when we least expect it and often as a result of what we least expect to educate us. If life is a surprise party, learning is too.

The cost for learning usually becomes more expensive when we're paying no mind. Life is tough; and tougher when we're stupid. I was out of town recently and hungry. It was early morning, and I found myself at a small restaurant called El Indio having huevos rancheros. The food was unpretentious and perfect. In my traditional enthusiasm for great grub I laced the eggs with too much of the house special salsa. Suddenly a small circle of fire ignited at my scalp line and moved south. As I began to sweat I also laughed, out loud. Here I was, out of school and a grown man, setting myself aflame in a Mexican restaurant just as I had done to myself so many times before. When, I wondered, would I learn? And then it dawned on me. Life is graduate school, and, *ay caramba,* we're all enrolled.

When I went to high school and college, students used to have to "run" for classes. You would race from room to room and try to get the class you "had to have," the professor who was a legend, or the course that was a "mick," as in Mickey—duh!—Mouse. But in life's graduate school, you don't have to "run" for classes. We're all already enrolled. Time will teach us that we have no idea what we've signed up for, and life's lessons certainly don't wait for us to sign up for the learning to begin. In life, as often as we run toward experiences we are just as often run over by them. Step off the curb in life without looking and, hello, learning can hit you like a truck.

The word *surprise* comes from the Old French and means at its root "to be taken from above." What surprises us is, by definition, a hand reaching out from nowhere and yanking our chain. But like the guy who wakes up every morning with hair on his pillow and is surprised one day to find he is bald, most of what surprises us is what we've been ignoring. In life there are fewer surprises than lapses of attention.

To find wisdom we only have to go in search of our ignorance. All learning begins not with what we know but by focusing our attention on what we don't know. Life is not a test, but we are all tested. Testing in schools is too often a system of tension disguised as learning. GPAs and SATs and GREs matter, but to be admitted to life's great graduate schools doesn't necessarily require great grades. It does demand the following: Look for your blindness. Listen for your deafness. Learn of your ignorance. And as the prophet Micah reminded: "Walk humbly . . ."

Years ago when I was invited to speak somewhere, I would feel compelled to pack up my wisdom and carry it on stage. Like a venerable Santa I would stumble under my supposed sack of sagacity toward the dais. This was necessary, I reasoned, because people had heard that I was smart, and purchasing the flattery I was burdened by my own notion of self. In life's graduate school I've discovered you don't need a book bag. Learning isn't something you have to "schlepp." Life is seldom heavy until we attempt to carry it. Ego is a burden; learning lifts.

Being clever doesn't mean we're not slow learners. Sometimes it takes a long time to learn we're not that smart. It took me several years in life's graduate school to learn this. And I still haven't graduated. What I have graduated to is coming to my public appearances responsible only for bringing my ignorance, my deafness, my blindness, and a willingness to go exploring with my audience. When we start from what we don't know, won't hear, or refuse to see, learning is a whole new territory.

"I wish I didn't know now," sang Bob Seger, "what I didn't know then." In life's graduate school you learn that once you have seen something you can't give away what you have seen. Innocence cannot be achieved; it can only be lost. And almost every transforming experience is accompanied by yet another loss of innocence.

When we are young, what we are hoping for is the wisdom to find our way. As we grow older, what we're praying for is the strength to carry on. In our rush to know much, we might be wise to remember that once our train leaves innocence the tracks don't run back. In life's graduate school we can learn what we don't know, but we can't unlearn. Some of us have a passion to know, but the passion to know can be a pain. There is much in life that we come to be sorry for knowing. If you doubt this, ask Adam and Eve. And still, even as doctors can tell us what to do, it is pain that we listen to. And some of life's lessons hurt, a lot.

Even the gentle lessons can leave scars, and tears falling long enough can scar rocks.

"Pride cometh before the fall," says scripture, and many of us have the scars on our knees to show for our hubris.

In life's graduate school it is only a fool who has never felt like one.

Those of us who take too much pride in our learning might want to think again.

In life's graduate school there are savants and fools, and sometimes it's tough to know the players without a roster. I know, I have been a dean and a dunce.

"Who is more foolish," asks the old quip, "the village fool or the one who argues with him?" In life's graduate school people don't necessarily graduate on schedule. In fact, there is no schedule and no one actually ever graduates. Anyone who thinks he or she has graduated from learning needs to go back to school.

In life's graduate school people can get honors and still flunk. In life you don't necessarily have to ask people what their grade point average is. You can see it in their lined brows, or the sag in their shoulders, or in the sunbeams dancing in their smiles.

In life's graduate school nobody gets straight A's. Except for trying.

I knew some guys in college who spent more time trying to figure out how to cheat than they spent studying. It's the same in life's graduate school. And people generally get about the same results.

Great cheaters become just that.

Most of us cheat a little, but the thought of being a "little cheat" makes our skin crawl. In biology class we learn that a snake grows by crawling out of its skin. In life's graduate school we learn it's tough to crawl out of our own skin. You can't cheat at growing up.

—•—

A grown-up is a contradiction in terms.

We are all growing ups.

———•———

Life's graduate school is a campus of contradictions. The campus is huge. It's the universe. And it's invisible. It's our mind, and our heart, and our soul. And the classes are huge. The whole world is in attendance.

But while classes are huge in life's graduate school, we all learn in ones. Life's most penetrating lessons are not learned in a crowd. Who among us has not at one point or another felt most done in life's crowd?

In life's graduate school we all learn that none of us can be found who have not felt lost.

"You cannot create experience," said the French philosopher Albert Camus, "you can only undergo it." Learning can happen in schools. It certainly happens out of school. I'm out of school and enrolled in Finding Faith 101.

There are 350 verses in the Bible directing how the ark, a box-like structure, should be built to hold the Ten Commandments, while there are only 31 verses describing how God created the world. Instructions for how to make a box take more than ten times the description necessary to convey the creation of the cosmos. Heaven knows, we're not very bright. But we're all enrolled in life's graduate school. And we're all learning.

And God isn't done with us yet. You learn that in Finding Faith 101.

We're all in a process of change, whether we are moving on from school or middle age or to forgetting how old we are.

Change is about finding our place in a new place.

Whether we are graduating from high school, college, or a life sorrow, tomorrow need not be framed by yesterday. Every day affords us a new canvas. We can borrow pigment and brushes from earlier artists, but each of us is an artist if we will dare to treat ourselves as no less. How the paint on our painting is applied matters, so we must apply ourselves. Each of us is a work of art, but we are a work in process.

Life has depths that only time explores.

Time does not wait for us to learn one lesson before it moves us on to the next.

Reality is only a memory ahead of its time.

Be cautious of arriving too early and missing what will later be waiting for you.

Sometimes looking backward is the best way to see ahead.

Each moment graduates to the next.

———◆———

Every degree is taken by degrees.

Behind great leaps are baby steps, baby steps.

———◆———

We can move mountains if we move one rock at a time.

———◆———

Because each of us is alone on our journey, we sometimes pack our fears for company.

Fear is a hitchhiker. Be cautious of who you pick up along the way.

———

Time, we learn, is a river and a river never walks; it always runs.

All moments are memories waving goodbye from the time we meet them.

———

Life is a surprise party; the invitations are in the mail.

Destiny does not need a forwarding address.

———

Sometimes the only way to find our way through blinding storms is with blind faith.

Memories are the way we mark time. And are marked by time. And memory is the gentlest of truths.

Be patient with yourself. Only time can open a rose.

———

3

Addressing Conflict

We are more often aggressive than courageous. And often confuse the two.

Fears on the inside often translate as anger on the outside.

Anger locks us in our house and then burns down the house.

Sadly, some of us have little but our anger to keep us warm.

We too often wear anger to mask our fears.

To face our fears, we first have to take off the mask.

Getting in touch with our anger is very different from being in its grasp.

Rabbi Nachman of Bratslav said, "God is present whenever a peace treaty is signed."

There is courage and heroism in planting and nurturing peace even if it is a fruit that will ripen after we have run out of seasons.

Peace can be watered by tears, and prayed for through pain, as long as it is nurtured with the faith of expectation.

Those who humbly do the right thing can take pride in helping set things right.

Many of us who bear the load are seldom burdened by praise.

———

Some who have chased success have instead found success in finding peace.

———

Too many of us live our life as reaction. And live our lives in reaction syndromes. Too bad. Too sad. Respond; don't react.

A third-grade teacher who read my thought above, responded by writing me and saying, "When you respond you ride the crest of the wave, and when you react you get caught in the undertow."

Our only insurance in life is not an insurance company that assures us we're in good hands, but seeing to it that our children are in good hands. In the hands, for example, of teachers who respond rather than react.

For many of us life is one long reaction syndrome. Things are coming at us so fast and furiously we feel like a pool ball careening from one side of the table to another, barely settled before we get creamed again and sent heading hopelessly into another ball that in turn is slamming us into a cluster of others. Life is not exactly a game of pool, but in our actions we often find we're reacting, not acting, and before we know it we're sunk. The shooter may call his or her shots in pool, but the ball don't say nothin'.

Physicists tell us that for every action there is a reaction. If this is true in space, then it is also true in the individual. And in the community. And among nations. And this truth has a consequence with its own gravity. We are weighed down as much by what is done to us as by what we do.

If we know that for every action there is a reaction, and we are subject to this, then we have a chance to lay out our next shot on the pool table by seeing where a reaction will take us. We can also see where responding rather than reacting will take us. We may be the raft, not the river, but we can steer.

We often steer ourselves into difficulty by spending too much time reacting to others. When we respond to our needs, we spend less time reacting to others.

I heard a television evangelist tell her audience, "Forgiveness is a lifestyle." Well, amen sister. Ain't that the truth. Perhaps if we responded to our needs, to our fears, to our hurts rather than reacting to them, perhaps then we would find forgiveness in our heart for ourselves. It may not be polite at the dinner table to help yourself first, but at the inner banquet no one can help others until they help themselves. People who are not self-forgiving cannot be other-forgiving. And until we are other-forgiving, we will not be divinely forgiven.

Once we get used to responding to our needs rather than reacting to our symptoms, we will do better in the larger pool game of life. When we are responding more often than reacting, we will be less a case of mindless velocity and vector. When we are responding more often than reacting, we will be less of a careening ego who will sink him- or herself before ever sinking a shot.

Responding rather than reacting gives us a little looser fit in life. Cut others a little slack and your own life gets a little more comfortable. Athletes are always told to stay loose. Loose is also good if you're working on being a better person, a jazzier jazz musician, or simply working at getting older with grace. Anger is part of life. It just isn't the best part. Anything worth being angry about will still be worthy of anger after we've cooled off. Nine times out of ten we're better for counting to ten. Sometimes ten times better off.

We all have a little of the farmer in us—most of our problems are homegrown.

William Hoy was an incredible baseball player. He played in the late nineteenth century and once threw three men out from center field in one game. He was also deaf. Most of the signals used by umpires and coaches in modern baseball were born out of Hoy's hearing teammates' efforts to communicate what the "count" was, who was safe, and who was out. Whether we're telling a player to steal second base or explaining to a suitor why they're not going to get past second base, hand signals help get the message across. Ironically, many of us who can hear miss the signals sent by others. And who among us has not made a mistake on the signals we have sent others?

When we make a mistake with our signals on the highway or on the highway of life, we incur not only the possibility of engaging someone's wrath but being in a wreck.

The nature of communication mixed with the anxieties and complexities of human psychology make for an anger minefield. And as a result we are often emotionally blowing up or blown away. Holding our tongue, thinking about what we are about to say, or actually saying what we're feeling rather than reacting to what is hurting, requires reins not spurs. Of course, some of us take pride "in always telling it like it is" and have, because of hubris, given up the effort to distinguish between what is honest and what is caring. Some of us use honesty as an aggressor and falsely compliment ourselves that we're not being aggressive but rather taking the ethical high ground.

Expressing one's anger is different from being an angry person. The philosopher Alfred Whitehead said, "Every truth is a half-truth." For any piece of good advice, there is a countervailing piece of good advice. "Those who truly guard the state are the teachers," says the Talmud. And the Talmud also reminds us, "Don't live in a city run by scholars."

"In the end, life is always a gag," said Charlie Chaplin. And clever as this line is, it is a truth that is a half-truth. Life is not always a gag. Or a party. Ask the victims. Life is not always a party unless you include fireworks, and little wars, and big wars, and war parties.

Nations are extensions of the individual and the community of individuals. Nations like the rest of us often react rather than respond. National cemeteries are filled with the tragic reaction pattern of nations. "Men and nations," said the Israeli statesman Abba Eban, "behave wisely once they have exhausted all the other alternatives."

Reactions are hurried wrong answers.

Make a response, rather than a reaction, your first choice rather than your last. And let us, as nations, do the same.

———•—

Life is short, too short to be short with others or ourselves. Before we have exhausted ourselves with reaction after reaction, let's pause and try on the line of Dr. Seuss's *Horton the Elephant:* "I said what I meant, and I meant what I said." Think if what you're saying is what you're meaning. Think if being mean is what you're meaning. Take a moment before you react. All of us can afford to. None of us can afford not to. If you think you don't have time to think before you act, think again.

When someone tries to give you their anger, be honest. Remind them this anger is theirs and not yours and there is no way you can take what doesn't belong to you.

———•—

The best way to lose our way is to lose our temper.

The best way to find our way is to really lose our temper.

———•—

4

⪻━━◈━━⪼

Aging, Loss, and Condolence

Change is the only constant.

Life is a going-away party from the moment we arrive at the party.

It's not that we lack for good advice in the face of change. It's just that advice about change seldom calms anxieties any more than reason necessarily puts fears to rest.

In a hurricane of change it's nice to have a basement. Find out who you are at your foundation.

When we are born we spend the first part of our lives trying to grasp the size and colors of the painting we've been painted into. As we grow older we begin to identify places and people. We begin to make a home from our frame of reference. What we soon learn, however, is that over time the painting, our painting of our world, is not a painting. It is a jigsaw puzzle. And pieces are being removed. People and places are leaving. Holes are being born in the world we just got to know. We go to sleep a continent and wake up an island. We grow older and find ourselves cut adrift without ever having left home.

Change always delivers; it just doesn't always deliver what we expect.

Desire often uses expectation to arrive at despair.

Some of us don't have the courage to suffer happiness.

Sometimes we move along and sometimes we're shoved along.

It was the philosopher Chamfort who said, "Man arrives as a novice at each stage in his life." Honor the novice in you by welcoming each moment with the innocence of coming to each moment, the good and the bad, anew. Because that is all you can do.

We have a tremendous capacity to ignore or deny information that interferes with how we want to be seen by ourselves. We seldom run out of the ability to delude ourselves, and we serve our delusion just as it serves us.

Walking on the beach, I see a group of teenage boys running into the water with complete disregard of the cold or the tide. Next to them stands an old woman. She doesn't want to be splashed. She shies away from the boys' enthusiasm. She was "once" and the boys are "now." She catches my eye catching hers. "I used to do that once," she says pointing to the boys, "when I was a girl." I say nothing, but smile. The woman looks at me cautiously, and then, with daring outside of her own expectation, she takes off her shoes, lifts the hem of her skirt, and walks into the water. I stand on the sand and applaud. She turns to me, returning the smile, and bows.

Holding on to her skirt, the woman walked in the sea until she gave birth to waves.

—————

"Once" is a time in all of our lives. "Now" is the dance.

—————

Reality is a state of transformation.

We are coming, going, and becoming all at once.

—————

PACKING UP A LIFE

My uncle Mike was a boxer when he was a boy. He later sold newspapers on the boardwalk in Venice, California. For 40 years he was a fixture on the beach, and then they replaced the fixtures. My aunt Rae, my mother's sister, worked in the cashier's office for a string of department stores in Santa Monica. When she retired she was tired. They had no children. They are now in their eighties. They can no longer look after themselves. My aunt wants to take a streetcar home from the hospital. My uncle, who can't himself remember how to open a can of soup, reminds his wife that the streetcars haven't run for thirty years.

Mike, who would challenge me to hit him as hard as I could in the stomach, and Rae, who prided herself on never asking any-one for anything, are both now crying for help. Only they no longer have the voiced energy to be heard and have forgotten the words. They used to take my brother and me fishing on the Venice pier. The pier was long ago torn down. The people who took us there now also find themselves being dismantled, caught in the tides of time.

My mother found a small nursing home for Rae and Mike near where they used to live. They can share a room. Nice people look after them, and they are safe. When my son places their TV on top of the bureau, they stare at it absently. He wipes the screen with the back of his sleeve. As I bend to kiss my aunt good-bye she asks if I can take her home. "This is your home now," I say. "Oh," she says. "I will come and visit," I say. "Oh," she says.

Some old people are confused. But so are some young people. Most of us are surprised to discover that we are not who we were. And often confused about who we might become. Young people wake up and discover that while they slept time crept in and changed the way they thought, exchanged tight jeans for baggy flesh.

Back at her sister's old apartment, my mother sits exhausted. She stares at the walls and wonders what to take, what to throw away, and what to sell. "Store or sell?" is the question as item after item is raised, inspected, and relegated to one cardboard box or another. Faded hand-colored postcards from Catalina

Island rest in a pile next to stacks of disposable diapers. "The home doesn't cover the cost of diapers," says my mother. We begin to figure how many are necessary per day, per week. All of which leads us to the question: "How long?" And my mother's eyes again well with tears.

I wonder what my 15-year-old son is thinking, looking at this refuse. Adam has agreed to make the 200 mile journey and lend the scene strength, but does he see a harbinger of his responsibility to me in my mother's obligation to her sister? Does he suddenly realize that even an indestructible boy of fifteen will one day hit the wire? I pick up a pair of binoculars and offer them to him. "Uncle Mike won't be needing these to see the future," I say. My son declines. I wonder if he, like me, hesitates to touch some of the items out of the feeling of being infected by the dis-ease of growing old.

My generation was told never to trust anyone over thirty. And, none of us will ever see thirty again. All of us push our own propaganda, and with luck we live long enough to realize it is propaganda. Growing old is a challenge. The strength to grow is an issue at any age.

We help my mother and her husband sort and sift attitudes as much as things and then prepare to leave. They will spend the night in the apartment. My mother is already old. She isn't afraid of old age's infection. She is sad. "Go," she says. "It is not your time," she says, with her sigh. "Yet," I say, inside.

As Adam and I head up the coast on the way home, we watch the waves to our left but say nothing. "I love you, son," I tell him. "You too," says my son. The day is dying, but the moment holds. That's what you get, I think to myself. Moments. You can't store them. You can't sell them.

———

Aging is something that happens at every age.

———◆———

All of us have differenct weather in our life, but all of us weather it differently.

———◆———

The death of a child is a death out of season. And ages all of us.

———◆———

Too many of us live out of season. It is summer, but our passions have cooled. It is fall, but we worry about beginning to lose our leaves. It is winter, but the long nights scare us. Too many of us find ourselves feeling like May in December or January in August. We sit on the beach with our soul wearing a parka. We ski downhill smiling and continue downhill after removing our skis. When we are out of season, we feel our lives are out of sync.

We cannot control the seasons, although hardly a season goes by that someone doesn't make the effort. Rather than attempting to bring rain out of season or red tomatoes before their time, perhaps we can work on warming our chill, growing our caring, being a cool breeze rather than a lot of hot air.

Every season is its own wonder. And while life is not always wonderful, it is certainly filled with wonder.

———◆———

Leaving "sadness" takes effort but is good exercise.

Leaving sadness, we should choose something to wear that feels like us. Feels like we would like to feel.

Sadness is often a hand-me-down. Sadness is as often something we picked up from someone else as it is of our own choosing.

Sometimes we don't realize that we have a whole closet of emotions because we haven't looked in the closet for so long. We don't have to get dressed up to leave sadness, but part of leaving is knowing how many emotions we have to choose from. Wear a smile.

Children love to dress up in old clothes. It makes them feel grown up. It's not sad when children mimic their parents, but it is sad when our children mimic our sadness. We should be cautious about leaving old sadness lying around. It is despairing to watch children slip into their parent's past sadness and ask, "How do I look?"

Leaving sadness requires us to give up the claim checks we're holding on old baggage. When we find ourselves feeling emotionally vulnerable, we often fling open our old suitcases and slip into some out-of-season anger, regret, or sadness.

The nature of sadness is to cry for our attention. Too often the way we respond to our sadness is not by hugging it but by embracing it as a life partner.

Say "so long" to sadness. A journey to a thousand smiles starts with the first one.

———

We all live in disappearing worlds. No matter who we are, soon it will be who we were.

We may know our lives by the interior photo album we've pasted in our heart. But in life there are no still photos, only movies. Life is on the move.

The past is often around the corner dressed as the future. How things will work out in the future will depend mostly on how we work on ourselves.

Life isn't Las Vegas but you couldn't be sure from looking at the bettors. Many of us are wagering we have enough time to waste it. Bad bet. We can't keep time, but we should think twice about throwing it away.

Like life, time is a surprise party.

At my 50th surprise birthday party, I saw people I hadn't seen in a long time. I passed a face in the mirror that looked older than the boy I knew myself to be.

We're all wondering when our parents are going to come home and tell us to take off time's costume. It's important not to forget this. It's important not to forget who we were. This has less to do with protecting the past and more to do with reminding us that we are a process.

Our character's challenge is not to spend too much time defending who we are in our current role. Tomorrow the Divine Director hands out new parts. She gets aches. He gets gray hair. We all get older. If we're lucky.

As often as not we use birthdays to give birth to expectation. We expect to be older. We expect to act older. We become what we expect. Perhaps we ought to take a candle off the cake each year as we get older. Perhaps we would grow younger.

Birthdays are an invitation to let time fly. Over time the challenge is not only what we can save but what we also can let go.

Instead of seeing birthdays as taking us one step closer to having our candle blown out, let us see birthdays as a way of lighting candles against the darkness.

———◦———

There are pains enough in life without us having to be a pain.

Pain does not use language to make its point. Indeed, when pain speaks, it is we who are left gasping for words.

———◦———

Pain points. It tells us to pay attention and where to pay attention.

Pain doesn't always show up on the X-ray screen.

Pain is its own isolation. Those in pain are cut adrift from those who are not in pain. There are two worlds when we are in pain—us and everyone else.

———◦———

Knowing our pain, we might find our role in it. Sometimes our pain is one of the few long-term relationships we know. We detest its presence and yet know ourselves by its company. Sometimes courage is asking our company to leave. Health is often deciding its time for pain to leave.

Telling people in pain, "I know you can deal with this," places burden on top of pain. We should allow friends to buckle under their load. It is enough to support one's pain without having to support the pretense of how strong others think we are. Offer friends in pain, and out, the right to be as strong as they think they are.

None of us have a prayer of getting out of here without pain. All of us can discover prayer as a path through the pain. Amen.

We are often not only the source of our own pain but also our own healing.

Few feel as abandoned as those who are sick in mind and spirit. This pain often has demons we do not want to discuss and that those who listen cannot cure.

Let us love those for whom love is the medicine they have been denied. Caring can cure.

Though dis-ease is often at the root of disease, every dis-ease is not a disease. Healing sometimes hurts. What's making us uncomfortable just might be making us see there is more than being comfortable.

What gives us comfort is not always a cure for what's ailing us.

Sometimes we can help those in pain. Sometimes it is our own hurting that causes us to hurt others. Sometimes what we think would heal others is what we need to heal in ourselves.

———◆◆◆———

We are our earthly vehicles. No vehicle runs on good intentions.

Taking care of others begins with taking care of ourselves.

———◆◆◆———

Life is an act in process, forever new even when our passing is the news.

People who are gone often come back to tell us they're okay. We're worried about them. And they're worried about us. Death has concerns for life as life has concerns about death. That we care for each other doesn't end when we drop our bodies. Bodies are often burdens. They inevitably become burdens for all of us. Not hearing from folks after they've passed away shouldn't necessarily be a cause for worry. Some people never called or wrote when they were here.

Death is not an insult. It is a reminder. People who are gone are not. Their spirit offers us a hand to higher places as we offer their spirit through memory a continued life in this world. This is the cosmic spiral. Elevators are running both directions.

Death is not the end of the line, because life is not a line. This is frustrating information when we want to see life as a race with beginnings, and endings, and medals, and pats on the back. If life is a race, it is a race forever in process.

—•—

Every beginning began as an ending, somewhere.

—•—

We don't know what to say when someone dies. When we don't know what to say, we tend to talk. Dead air makes us nervous. Telling people why they shouldn't be sad doesn't make them happy. Listening to people before they die and to those who have lost someone may be the higher part of saying anything.

In the presence of death we focus on "what we can do" because we can do little. By its nature death reminds us that we are not in control. Regarding death, "doing" is not our domain.

The Talmud stipulates that if a funeral procession meets a wedding party, the funeral should give way. Choose life over death, say the scriptures.

——◆——

Death can be a loss but is always a lesson.

Death threatens life no less than it gives it meaning.

We lose the most from death when we refuse to learn its lesson— the lesson of living: Live, love, and let go.

——◆——

5

Relationships

Love is like the hall pass you used to get in school.

Love allows us to go places we cannot go on our own.

Love is a ladder; it allows us to climb out of ourselves.

Some of us have fallen in love. Some of us have needed a little push.

Falling in love is just that. Falling, however, is very different from landing.

Lovers may fall from reason but seldom into reason.

Understanding love is a contradiction in terms.

———◦◦———

I pull into traffic and hear two songs in a row about love gone wrong. I wonder how many people are driving with their heart hurting. My eyes following my mind, I look at the driver in the lane next to me. It is a woman crying, and pounding the steering wheel. Suddenly, unintentionally, I'm prying, and I turn away. All of us have had those moments when we see more in someone then we intended to look at and they intended us to see.

There is the old wisdom that to fall in love you sometimes have to shut one eye, and to stay in love you sometimes have to shut both eyes.

People looking to remain in love learn that sometimes you have to look the other way.

People looking for love learn that sometimes you have to look in another way.

Every heart needs a set of blinds that can be opened and closed.

What's missing in our lives doesn't always miss a chance to speak to us.

Love doesn't always wait around to hear what we intended to say.

Little speaks more loudly than what isn't said.

———◦◦———

Love does not require a translator.

Love too often is lost in the translation to words.

———◆———

Words wound as often as they heal, but love is often its own curative language. And though love heals, the inverse is also true. When we have not been loving to ourselves in mind, body, or spirit, we are in pain. Or will be.

What was is reborn as what is. "Energy," according to physics, "cannot be created nor destroyed. It only changes form." Everything is in relationship.

What love was is different from what it becomes, and though much is lost, who can say whether more is not gained.

Love, like a shell tossing in the tide, is never lost but is always transformed.

———◆———

Our heart is a muscle. Our heart requires exercise or the muscle atrophies. Make being loving a daily workout.

———◆———

Heart and heartache share the same bed.

Sometimes we can be more loving by forgetting instead of forgiving.

When love listens, it listens to the heart, and with heart.

One can be wise about many things, but one doesn't want to be wiser than love.

Let us remember that we are alone together.

Caring helps us find our balance.

Not caring about others reflects that we have already lost our balance.

Not caring about ourselves is a guarantee that we will never find our balance.

It isn't just that women are redefining men, it's that men and women are both being redefined, and often neither can find the other without a dictionary.

Men and women need a place where they can get together but often stay together if they have a place where they can get away from each other.

Getting along with one another sometimes requires us to move along without one another.

Relationships need silences in order to make music together.

Unfortunately, in some relationships there is more silence than music.

———◦———

People in long-term relationships often feel that passion has fled. But that is often because we expect others to be the source of our passion.

It's usually we who have lost what we're trying to find in others.

Most of us listen to speak instead of listening to hear. We can't wait for others to stop talking in order to tell them what we think instead of thinking about what they're saying.

Listening to someone you love is often more important than what they have to say.

———◦———

PACKING PICKLES AND PROBLEMS

Doctors say there is enough salt in one pickle to give us all the sodium we need for a year. I'd like more years, so I consume fewer pickles. But this is a story I still gnaw on over the years. It is a story my father's mother told over and over. And over and over. When I was younger I thought this was just the malaise of her advancing age. But it wasn't. She was simply hoping we were listening.

The story goes that two or three times every year in the mid-summer, my grandmother and other ladies in the neighborhood would gather at one of their homes to pack pickles. They each brought a bushel of cucumbers, dill, salt, bay leaves, jars, and their troubles.

They always gathered at different people's homes but always around a large table. They would unload their bushel baskets, setting the ingredients before them. And then they would unpack their problems.

In turn and with respect, each of the women would begin to talk about what was wrong in her life. Who was sick. Who was still single. Who was getting older. Who hadn't slept with her husband. Who wished she hadn't. What couldn't be whispered on street corners found its way to the table. We are all gasping to breathe, and here there was airtime. Safe air. The tone was less gossip than confessional. The listening done with an ear to hear, to help. And no matter what was said, no matter the shouts of telling silences, a promise went into every jar with the pickles. A promise not to tell.

The conversation would last most of the afternoon and was punctuated by sips of hot tea from old jelly jars. Heads nodded with understanding as burdens were unpacked and pickles packed. Eyes rolled with disbelief at stories that would never leave the room. "Please God," they would nudge each other, "don't show me what I can bear."

At the end of the day, the women would stand and arch their backs. They would wash the coarse salt from their hands. They would slowly load their listening and jars of pickles back into the bushels they brought. Each of them would offer the others a feel of how heavy their bushel was. And then they would go home staggering under their load. Each with her own bushel.

Each a queen carrying her burdens with bearing. Each thinking of what she had heard.

At this point in the story my grandmother would lift her eyebrow and wag her finger so the lesson was not lost. Spirit to spirit, I want her to know I got the message. Caring impacts what we are carrying.

Every one of the women had arrived at the afternoon feeling weighted by her burdens. And then, each of them had heard the load that the others carried. Each of them had felt the weight of the other's bushel. And each had gone home thankful to be lugging only her own troubles. Thankful for what was hers. Even the anguish, and the aches. The load had shifted. Their lives seemed lighter without weighing any less.

We offer others a chance to lighten their load when we say little and listen loudly.

We learn a great deal about life and its burdens when we quietly help others to unpack theirs.

Our own burdens weigh less when we listen to what is weighing on others.

———————

6

Hopes and Fears

Hope is contagious. Its infection inspires. Let us come to each day with hope. Not because we should but because we can.

Rich and poor, let us teach our children to find hope in the details of living rather than in despair in their disappointed anticipations.

When children of the poor are asked what they want to do, the majority answer about their plans for that afternoon, that evening. That is the horizon of their hope. That is where their sea and sky meet. They do not sense there will be wind to sail farther when the world of opportunity is flat.

Only hope sits on the dock waiting for its ship to come in.

Only hope books passage from despair.

———•———

Over two thousand years ago, Cicero said: ". . . As long as there is life, there is hope." But kids who never learn to read don't read Cicero. Let us teach all kids to read hope in the future.

We cannot come to faith through reason. But we have every reason to have faith.

Hope is not arrived at by a good argument nor need be lost by one.

Hope doesn't always make sense. Often my heart knows what my mind only thinks it knows.

Reason may be reasonable, but on the high road to hope, reason is just another roadside attraction.

Praising hope does not refuse reason. It is rather to understand that reason, like money, can be a false god.

"To fear is to worship what you fear," said Rabbi Isaac Meyer of Ger in the eighteenth century. Do not sanctify your fears. Sanctify hope.

———•———

We become what we look for.

Look for hope, and we will look hopeful.

———•———

Social sanity is not agreeing that we are all watching the same movie, but that we are all sitting in the dark.

Our common insecurity and doubts make us all neighbors.

———•———

Fear is like the rich man who was carried everywhere. When asked if he could walk, he would answer, "Yes, but fortunately I don't have to." Why would our fears walk away when they have us to carry them?

———•———

Heroes are not people free of fears but rather people who are not framed by their fears.

To turn our lives into works of art we may only have to step out of the fears that frame us.

———•———

We're a sea of emotions and as often as not make the waves that swamp us. Harnessing our emotions may mean learning to ride our own waves.

———•———

The disturbing questions in life are no more real than the reassuring answers.

Do not fear your questions. Do not be falsely lulled by your answers.

———•———

"Mornings are wiser than evenings," goes an old Russian proverb. Often what appear as the 3 A.M. facts of life are in fact distractions.

If we go to a movie matinee and come out into the light, the light disturbs us. Coping requires us to remember that whatever "movie" we've been watching, we've been in the dark.

When our blindness is familiar, seeing can be frightening. Most of us are more prepared to cope with our blindness than with the prospect of seeing.

———•———

I heard an ad for a school in Nevada that teaches you how to deal cards. The six-week course prepares and guarantees you a job as a "dealer." I began to wonder if there were schools like that for the rest of us caught up in life's games and trying to deal with them.

Win, lose, or draw, we all need to deal with things until we have dealt with them. If problems are inevitably part of life's shuffle, then winning in life depends how we deal with what we're dealt.

———•———

There is a story drawn from Talmudic literature that answers why Noah released a dove to search for land after the flood. The story explains that the dove, when it tires, can rest one wing and fly with the other. This ability to fly with one wing affords the dove the capacity to travel huge distances. The mythic dove can be at dis-balance, give itself rest, and still carry on. Oh, that we could find that bird's character in our own.

If we want to look like heroic figures, we might remember that honesty in the face of fear is its own heroism. Strength isn't the absence of weakness but how we wrestle with our weaknesses.

———————

The issues that we move to the back burner can still burn us.

Things heat up every time we turn our back on an issue that requires us to face it.

Problems don't get put behind us because we show them our behind.

"Competing pressures tempt one to believe an issue deferred is a problem avoided; more often it is a crisis invited," said Henry Kissinger.

The world does not go into hiding when we shut our eyes.

———————

Mark Twain said, "I am an old man and have had many terrible problems, and most of them never happened." Often what's happening in a problem is that we are the problem.

Often things drive us nuts because we started out a little crazy. Stress tries to kill us 24/7. Get even. Lose the stress before you're lost. Lose the Velcro. Go Teflon. Let the stress that others lay on you slide off like two fried eggs in a Teflon pan.

———————

Life rains on all of us. Some of us are flooded by a neighboring river, some by guilt. When news of impending floods arrives, some of us give up, some of us pray, and some of us figure we have three minutes to learn to live under water.

In trying to cope with our emotions we should remember that emotions are tropical hurricanes. They blow over trees and then blow over.

——•—•——

7

Strength and Character

Shortly after my daughter learned to walk, her great joy was to knock me over. I would get down on my haunches, and she would race at me, and we would tumble together. I was to her a tower of strength and in tottering the tower she was stronger yet. My willingness to be less made her more. And I was more for it. We both knew we were playing. Time would change the game. Time always changes the game. Strength and character are time tested.

Fathers cannot always be stronger than their children, but can always be a source of strength.

People want to be seen in strength. We like to muscle up to others. We want to marry, in work and love, to strength. But even when we marry our strengths we have affairs with our fears.

The question is whether we have the strength to admit we are scared. We're not all tiptoeing around terrified, but all of us can feel our fears nibbling on us. Or in us.

Years ago there used to be comic book ads inspiring us to get strong because life bullies us and sometimes kicks sand in our faces. Whether we're building our body or simply trying to lift our spirits, it is the day-in and day-out dealing with the weights, pushing the gravity weighing on us, that is required.

Strength is achieved one workout at a time. Top body builders work muscle groups to exhaustion. Those of us who feel exhausted trying to deal with affairs of state or the state of our affairs should remember that in our exhaustion is future strength.

———

Life is double-stranded. Every strength has its inherent weakness.

We better like our strengths, because we're going to pay for them.

Sometimes we provide others the strength we cannot provide for ourselves. Lending strength makes us stronger.

———

Time is its own truth.

Memory is the gentlest of truths.

People have long snuggled with warm lies rather than lying down with cold facts.

We like our lies even when we don't like the fact that we're lying.

Sometimes we need to lie to ourselves just to get through the night. This need to lie is its own truth—our shared truth as people—our shared need to get through the night.

Sometimes we pray to convince ourselves of what we say we believe.

———•—•———

All of us have told ourselves lies we must believe for sacrifices we think are necessary.

———•—•———

In all of our lives there are fears bearing down on us. Or it feels that way. We are often separated from our fears only by tents we have pitched in the night. What transforms us into heroic characters is not a form-fitting Superman or Superwoman suit but the form of our character.

Character is seldom formed overnight, but often in the soul's dark night.

Greatness is rarely achieved when things are great.

———•—•———

Feeling good about ourselves doesn't mean that things are good.

The question for all of us is whether we feel good about how we're conducting ourselves no matter what is happening.

———•—•———

At some point we all conduct ourselves badly. This doesn't make us bad if it serves to remind us that we can do better.

In life there are no good conduct medals. Good conduct is its own reward.

We're all musicians conducting ourselves. In order to make great music we must keep an eye on the conductor. And the conductor must keep an eye on us. Sometimes we have to keep an eye on our character, and sometimes our character needs to keep an eye on us.

Sometimes later is too late.

What we stop doing is sometimes the most important thing we do.

Sometimes our biggest distractions are attractions.

The social lie of all time is trading truth for company.

To conduct ourselves on a "higher" level is not always an elevating experience.

We may not be the masters of our fate. We can be masters of our attitude in the face of fate.

A pearl begins in an oyster as a grain of sand that causes an irritation. The oyster's manner of dealing with this irritation transforms the sand into a pearl. Some of us feel our life will not be right until we rid ourselves of every irritation. But like the fairy tale princess who could feel a pea under a mountain of mattresses, the less discomfort in our lives, the more a single grain will be felt. Time and tides will bring grains of irritation into all of our lives. How we respond can transform what bothers us into what enriches us.

Problems are often pearls waiting to be appreciated.

I had a friend named Edith. When we met she was in her eighties. She was raised as a princess in Eastern Europe, and then the wheel turned. She and her parents had to flee for their lives, packing little more than memories in their luggage. Transformed by a world in transformation, she found herself at the age of twenty living in Detroit and bent over a sewing machine for twelve hours a day. She married but had no children. She grew old. Lost a husband. Moved to the West Coast. Baked strudel. And remembered. And was happy. Almost always. When I asked her the secret of her attitude, she laughed and answered, "When I was young, I looked around and realized that in this life you could be happy or sad." Edith shrugged her shoulders. "I decided to be happy."

Happiness can sometimes be a decision—as can unhappiness.

———

Innocence and sincerity have not entirely passed out of fashion but little today is fashioned from these character fabrics. Strange to think we might have become too sophisticated to be sincere, too emotionally experienced to be innocent.

Innocence is an attitude that makes us available. Attitudes that close us down bring us down.

———

A second chance is sometimes a chance to be right by admitting we were wrong.

As regards time, none of us are innocents; we are all guilty. After all, who among us cannot be found guilty of standing around just killing time.

———•———

Sometimes the only way to keep from drowning is to throw one's self into the sea.

Sometimes the sanest way to hang in is to let go.

———•———

Sometimes the only way to take away our fear's power is to acknowledge that we have given our fears their power.

———•———

Sometimes what we want badly serves us badly.

———•———

The simplest way to make the common profound is by appreciating the moment.

Almost all of us, and all of us when we're children, confuse our needs with our wants. The fact is that we all want. And we would all be better served by thinking long and hard on our "wants." Most of us were raised to sit down at the kitchen table and make a list of what we wanted out of life. Few of us take the time to sit down at the kitchen table and be thankful for what we have—including a kitchen and a table.

Taking stock of what we have in hand is more difficult for most of us than figuring out how to grab more.

My community is blessed with an incredible physical environment. The sunrise casts horizontal channels of red light across the horizon. On any given dusk, people line the borders of the beaches to watch the sunset. But if you want to see an incredible sunrise in any community, go to the front door of your local hospital and watch a smile dawning across the countenance of a mother going home with her child. If you want to see an incredible sunset go to the same hospital and watch the light refusing to fade in the face of an old man able to take his wife home so they can again sit together and talk by the fire.

We seldom remember what we promise we won't forget, while the "nothing" incident we barely noticed is already carved in our frontal lobes. We think we will best remember what we have spent the most time trying to acquire. That's why gratitude is such a gift of character. It teaches us how much we receive when we pause to say thanks for what we already have.

Gratitude is its own wisdom. Think about how smart we would be if we were too smart to say, "Thank you."

Character is a compass. Find the strength to use your compass and you will find your way. And find your way when you lose your way.

8

Passion
and Compassion

I have a friend who by the time he was fifteen knew he wanted to be a writer. Though he dated many different girls through high school and college, my friend had only one passion. Writing. He later met a wonderful woman, married, and has a beautiful family. Through it all, however, he has maintained this long-term "affair" with writing. His wife laughs that they have an "open marriage." He meets his passion late at night, over coffee in the mornings, and talks about "her" constantly. He does not ignore this lover for fear "she" will ignore him. His wife certainly doesn't want him to ignore "her." "She" nurtures him and feeds his family. "She" has introduced them to movie stars and last year paid for a new roof. "I'm not a religious man," he says now at middle age, "but I thank God for this passion in my life."

Finding our passion is a religious experience. Without passion we don't have a prayer. A life absent of passion is a vacuum that sucks the life from us.

Most of us understand passion less as something we possess than something we are looking for. We know it by its absence. We talk about absent passion as if it were a hat or a pair of sunglasses we left on a counter when we walked from a room. For many of us passion is the deeply felt hole in our lives.

Knowing something is missing is the first step toward finding it. That passion is missing in our lives doesn't mean passion is absent.

Searching for passion is sacred work. As in so many other areas, the search as much as the solution transforms us—if we search passionately.

It's never too early to be in pursuit of one's passions and never too late to guard them.

Passions are pursuing us as often as we are chasing them.

———◆———

People with passion tend to magnetize the rest of us. We are drawn to passion. Even if it is not ours.

We like to be in the proximity of passion. We want to warm our hearts in its glow.

———◆———

To find our passion doesn't mean we have to start a fire. We only have to find our fire.

To find our fire begins by leaning toward what warms us. Inside each of us is the kindling to stoke our own fire.

———

To go fishing for your passion, you have to cast with your heart.

———

We can find reasons to be passionate, but reason is not passion's bait.

Be passionate about fishing and let others worry about what you catch.

———

Passion is its own success. Even failing can be successful if the effort has been passionate.

———

Passions are all quicksilver and shadows. Unlike Peter Pan, we cannot sew our passions to us. Passions are not stitched to our schemes, but to our visions.

Passions come and go when they like. Passions do not like curfews.

Passions require special handling and are passionate about how they are handled. Strangely, passions are sensitive but not fragile. Passions are vulnerable and invincible. Passions wound easily and die hard.

———

I have found my passion. And lost it. I have found it again. And lost it once again. Welcome to the planet Earth. We walk on a giant ball. Losing our balance is part of the journey. I have found myself being passionate about things that don't matter. And guilty of assuming that now-absent, ignored passions would always grace my company.

Passions are more than momentary lust. Lust is luscious but we seldom want more lust than a bellyful.

Passions are more than something you want, or must have. They are something that have you.

Ask your passion for a date. It may turn into the affair of a lifetime. It's not now or never, but now is never again.

———◆———

To be compassionate literally means to live with passion.

Compassion is almost always a prescription for anyone in pain—and certainly for anyone whose pain is the absence of passion.

When Mother Teresa's fame grew, she was inevitably asked her opinions on love, and faith, and work. People wanted to hear what she had to say and wanted to pass her words along. Unsure what to do with this attention, Mother Teresa's response was usually as loving as it was terse: "There should be less talk . . . take a broom and clean someone's house. That says enough."

It was the famed violinist Jascha Heifetz who said, "Man is usually trying to make something for himself rather than something of himself."

———◆———

Love and work are the balance points in life. If we're fortunate, we love our work. If we're wise, we'll work at love.

While most of us work to feed ourselves, there is always work available that any of us can do to feed our spirit. The difference between the labors of heaven and of hell may simply be whether we're sweeping others out of our way or picking up a broom to sweep another's room. Any of us looking for a good job can probably think of a good deed that needs doing.

———

"There must be more to life than having everything," wrote the children's author Maurice Sendak. There is. There is having less. And there is the knowledge that having more will make us happy only more or less.

Working for ourselves is good work. And it is the first work that needs to be done. But there are also labors in life that will reward us long after we have everything and will enrich us even when we have less. A labor of love is work that is always at hand.

We can't be underpaid for a labor of love because this work makes our life richer.

A labor of love doesn't make sense, and its glory is in not making sense.

A labor of love is about giving, not taking, and getting more than we're giving. A labor of love isn't about making a great deal but reshuffling the deal for those who were dealt less. Life isn't a game if you're always the loser. Look at the cards you're holding and think about what you might do for those who got lost in the shuffle.

Be passionate about compassion and about self-compassion. The first person we might treat to a labor of love is our self. If that sounds greedy, you might be just the candidate who needs some love but never allows yourself to ask for what you need. Sometimes a labor of self-love is reminding ourselves that we like who we are just the way we are, and having more won't mean we love ourselves more. Any more than having less will cause us to think less of ourselves.

There is a Hebrew proverb that says: "No one tries to steal your troubles, and no one can take away your good deeds."

No one.

Sometimes there is nowhere that love takes more labor than with the self. No one else can take away our right to love ourselves even though a lot of us give away what can't be taken away.

The best way to measure a society to see whether it is civilized is by noting how those with power treat those without power. Labors of love make us, both as individuals and as a society, more powerful because they remind us that we are stronger for being a source of strength to others.

Laborers are strong. Labors of love strengthen the heart. Lifting weights builds muscle; lifting others builds character. Work out. Helping others to lift themselves is the best workout.

Orphan children are seldom heard asking for help. That doesn't mean they're not asking. It does mean that no one is generally listening.

It is a labor of love to listen to kids. Any kid. The labor part is sitting on our adult need to talk, and tell, and direct. Love is listening when we would love to hear our own voice. Quieting our need to be important is a labor of love that shouts for attention.

Parenting is a labor of love. It is being loving without expectation.

Do not kiss your children so they will kiss you back, but so they will kiss their children and their children's children.

—•—

Parenting is compassion that is a guaranteed underpaid, under-appreciated job that is the best job anyone can get. Lots of people can have children. Being a parent is letting the child have you. Every parent is a working parent. Any parent who isn't working at being a parent will soon be working on problems.

Parenting is a labor of love that sometimes seems like all labor until you get paid. With love. Parenting is a labor that sometimes makes you feel like you don't matter until you learn that the chance to love your child is all that matters.

People who adopt kids sometimes have problems. Of course, so do people who give birth to kids. Orphans aren't just kids without parents. They are also kids who are orphaned from love. My mother spent years in an orphanage and later found the love she never had by giving love. Any of us looking for love might find giving love difficult. But if giving love is a labor, and it can be, the giving makes it a labor of love.

—•—

Friendship is compassionate caring. A friend is someone who will help us work through our stuff and call it a labor of love. A labor of love isn't a friend who labors to be right but someone who reminds us of our right to be who we are.

A labor of love is a friend who will stay with us through the long night when we're in labor giving birth to ourselves.

———◆———

Compassion is taking the time to visit people in hospitals, taking a grandparent out for the afternoon, visiting a gravesite, lending someone your car, washing a friend's car, wishing your old boyfriend or girlfriend well, listening to a stranger, listening to a story you've heard a thousand times one more time, leaving groceries anonymously for someone who is poor, giving to charity, giving of yourself charitably.

We all get caught up in our lives. We are all poor actors who strut and fret on the pinhead of a moment and then are gone. Compassion in action, however, is a labor of love that lingers longer than we do. Let compassion be the melody that lingers after you.

———◆———

There is more to life than loving, but little that isn't lovingly done can be called living.

Life is a labor. Make it a labor of love. It is work that will work for you.

Remarkably, giving compassion will bring more passion to your life.

Giving a damn can make our life worth a damn.

———◆———

9

———◆———

Looking Inward

Rather than meeting ourselves or others for who we are, we tend to turn ourselves into drive-in movies. We project onto our social-screens how we want to be seen and walk around in character wondering why people don't see the "real" me.

———◆———

We are the painter, the paint, and the painting.

———◆———

Though remembering who we were is important, sometimes forgetting, even for a moment, cuts us the slack to become who we would like to be.

Most of us remind each other not to forget where we came from and forget that a friend is also someone who reminds us of who we might yet become.

———

"Realists" like to say that there is no free lunch.

Economists will tell there is a cost to everything.

In the economics of self, the cost of who we are is always established by measuring ourselves against who we might be.

———

"Cherish forever what makes you unique," said Bette Midler, "'cuz you're really a yawn if it goes."

"Fitting in" in life can be lonely business. Fitting rooms tend to be for one person at a time. You can come out and ask the sales clerk or your friends what they think, but even if they're telling you the truth, it's their truth.

Finding where we fit means stepping back from others and being self-verifying.

———

To make the world different begins with knowing we make a world of difference.

———

What others know about us may matter.

What we know about ourselves definitely matters.

———◆———

Dealing with others begins with how I'm dealing with me.

The titles of the roles we play in life shift and are at best handles rather than definitions. Defining who we are is not the defining issue. Being who we are is.

———◆———

Until we can embrace our own company, it's doubtful that we'll feel the joy that comes from fitting in with others.

One's own company is good business once you find it. To fit in we need to go in, inside ourselves. Fitting in begins inside of us.

———◆———

The way ahead is the path within.

———◆———

I once went to a small town carnival that had a room filled with mirrors. Each mirror had a different distortion. Depending on where you stood you could be tall or short, fat or thin. You could pick how you wanted to see yourself by deciding the mirror you chose to stand in front of. If you stayed in the room long enough you would have no idea if any of the mirrors were honest. You would have no idea what you really looked like. And we do this all the time. Only instead of paying a quarter, we pay with our lives. The consequence of where we take our reflection is that we often make decisions on what fits—work, husbands and wives, lives—by looking in mirrors that parade lies we've asked to see. Each of us contains a hint of the dark queen in Snow White who demands her mirror fit her image.

We not only look in mirrors, we are mirrors.

It is the nature of polite society to mirror each other. We are mirrors posing in front of mirrors. The confusion is infinite, and we like it. We spend our days seeing ourselves in others who are seeing themselves in us.

Almost all of us are less often looking for what fits us than for what flatters us.

When we're looking for someone to come out and play, let's not forget to knock on our own door.

"Every man," said Emerson, "supposes himself not to be fully understood or appreciated."

Many of us mine others as excuses for lives we never live.

At the end of our days, what do the excuses matter?

Certainly there are sorrows that are real and not imagined. But, we sometimes make what isn't real real, what is sort of real more real, and what could be real real all because we want the emotional rush of feeling sorry for ourselves.

We all like to pet ourselves and say things like, "It'll all be okay." [It all won't.] "You don't deserve this." [If we got what we deserved, it might be worse.] Very few of us find that what we'd like is what life is like. Like it or not.

What often insults our ego is when things don't work out the way we projected things were supposed to go. We're usually so upset about our plans being upset, and so enamored with the self-pity, we can't see if what did happen is positive. Once we've made up our mind to be self-pitying, we don't like to be disturbed with the facts. Even while somewhere in the universe they are playing an old Country Western song that reminds us that some of God's greatest gifts are unanswered prayers.

The challenge for all of us is to work with what we're given. Almost all of us argue with our portion. For some of us it is an issue of size, and for some it is an issue of substance. Some of us have been served scraps and some of us are anxious to scrap no matter what we've been served. All of us serve ourselves excuses.

There is a timeless story that reminds us that the difference between heaven and hell is not the size of the portions but that in hell people never seem to have enough to feed themselves and in heaven people somehow always have enough to feed their neighbors.

Don't make the next party you throw yourself a pity party.

We don't need an excuse to cry or need to be excused. Just like at family amusement parks where they have orchestrated "camera-stops" as places to stop and snap, in life, too, there are view sights where the situation suggests we stop and weep. And we should. And then we should move on. There is more to see. Other rides to ride.

Have the courage to look into who you are and no matter what you see, you'll also see your courage.

Look into who you are and chances are your outlook on life will be looking up.

10

Finding Peace

Hope for the best; make peace with the rest.

Any peace we find in life is its own blessing, and any blessing that does not bring us peace is no blessing.

A century ago men used to whittle in front of the General Store. Jokes were told, life was examined, and pretense was out-lawed. When you really want to understand what's important, sometimes you've just got to take out the old penknife and peel the bark off of a moment.

An eternity is any moment opened with patience. And patience is the doorway to peace.

Peace is just below the surface. If you're looking for peace, you may need to peek beneath your surface.

When the info/techno/cyber world closes in, a lot of men feel a need to mount up and ride out to the garage. There they can cuddle in the chaos of dried-up paint cans filled with nails, oily rags, and old bicycles. This is not a clubhouse. It is better. It's a mess. "My mess," says a man admiring his surroundings.

Women are as often organizing a mess as men are making a mess of an organization. What's important is that we all need a corner, a place to "putter."

For most men this is not generally a place with a tablecloth and a coaster. But, it doesn't make you a real man to have a dirty garage any more than having a clean home makes you a real woman.

What's really important to all of us is a sense of place, because peace of mind is often hand in glove with a place of peace.

———•———

We are all well advised not to waste time. Some of us, however, waste time by always being busy.

Certainly there is indolence in lazing, but the Romans were industrious, corrupt, and are now history. And if industry was a sign of character, a few losing characters would have won the wars they started.

Making peace is always good work.

———•———

To relax doesn't necessarily mean we're being lax. To relax is the first step in finding peace.

Most of us find finding peace a little difficult. Almost all of us find losing peace painful.

————

Peace between nations is the absence of war. Peace for a person is often when we stop waging war on ourself.

There is courage and heroism in planting peace even if it is a fruit that will ripen after we have run out of seasons.

Peace can be watered by tears, and prayed for through pain, as long as it is nurtured with the faith of expectation.

————

Some who have chased success have found their reward in finding peace.

When we offer others harbor, we calm our own storms.

Peace is found only by those who are looking for it, or have wearied of overlooking it.

————

"He does not seem to me to be a free man," wrote Cicero, "who does not sometimes do nothing."

Recreation should be more than working at hedonism. Recreation at its highest is a time for re-creation. And nothing important ever began that didn't begin by calming the mind and spirit. Finding peace is the first step to helping find our path.

Sometimes the most important thing we can do is what we don't do. Being in a state of peace with the world is not a state of inaction. Don't confuse being peaceful with doing nothing.

———•••———

In the social revolution of the 1960s, a world of new words was born. In the 1960s young people used language as a way to make claims about the world and claim self. Parents complained they couldn't understand their kids, and kids liked it that way. In the 1960s we didn't want to be understood, we wanted to say something. Often shouting.

Ideas are contagious. Language makes ideas airborne. One of the lasting terms out of that period is the word *uptight*. We called our parents and teachers "uptight."

The term uptight, while it probably didn't do much for world peace, did serve to remind some and accuse others that they, indeed we, were not at peace. In this regard, the 1960s still live. We live in a world where tension is our "breakfast of champions." Few of us start our day without a little tension.

For some of us our daily tension is served cold. Perhaps some-one treats us a little chilly. For some of us it's served hot. Perhaps someone treats us to a little anger.

Some people think tension is good for you. They say tension is Mother Nature's way of keeping us on our toes. Perhaps, but then tension also has too many of us slugging it out toe to toe.

Most of us have some leisure time, but many of us when we take our leisure don't find ourselves feeling relaxed. "The secret of being miserable," said George Bernard Shaw, "is to have the leisure to bother about whether you are happy or not."

The term *relax* is from the Latin *laxare,* to loosen. When we tell people to stop being so "uptight," what we're telling them to do is "loosen up." Telling people to "loosen up" usually brings them down.

For some of us feeling "uptight" means we're shipshape, taut, in control. For others of us these attitudes imply we're out of control because of our need, well . . . to be in control.

Little makes us more "uptight" than when we find things out of our control. The fact that we are the raft, not the river, is hard news for any of us who like to brag about being captain of our fate.

This doesn't mean we don't have to paddle, row, and steer, but it also means that sometimes the best way to captain our ship is to forget about trying to steer, and to pick up a rod and go fishing. Fishing is also work; it's just that it's usually the fish that get worked. Of course there are a few fisherman who thought fishing was fun but could swear they heard the fish laughing.

Art Linkletter loved to tell of a little boy who complained to his mother about having to take his little sister with him when he went fishing because the last time he took her he didn't catch anything. "Well," said his mother reassuringly, "if you explain to your sister that she needs to be quiet, she will."

"Oh, that's not the problem;" said the boy, "she ate the bait."

In life, success is the bait and most of us take the hook. Love, power, fame, and vanity are also in the bait box. Every now and then it's a good meditation to see ourselves standing on the shore watching ourselves in the stream, circling life's hooks and making sure we want what we're about to bite on. Sometimes it takes great skill and effort to catch ourselves. Just in time. And calm down. And make peace with ourselves.

"Every river has its own course," said Rabbi benHiyya in the Talmud, and it is an Asian wisdom that reminds us, "You can't push the river." Of course we all know this, and even those of us who don't know it will in the course of our lives come to learn it. Life often takes less effort and more patience. And for many of us finding peace can not only be hard, it can be hard labor.

Sit peacefully on the bank of the river long enough in life and everything will float past you. You don't always catch what you're fishing for, and who among us hasn't sometimes caught more than we bargained for. Sometimes we fish for wealth and land character. Sometimes we fish for faith and hook hope.

When someone hangs up a sign that says "Gone Fishing" they're usually not calling it quits—just calling it a day. Or maybe an hour. Sometimes walking away from something is the best way to approach it. Sometimes stepping back from our efforts can draw us closer to our goals. Give people a little breathing room and they may want to get a little closer to you.

Some of us feel we've had our fill. Some of us aren't happy no matter how full we are. Some days, when the world feels like elevator doors are shutting on us, just the thought of calling it quits sounds like a mountain brook with the brown trout running. Some days we need to hang a "Gone Fishing" sign on our self-expectations and teach our career to cast and wait quietly.

Water behind a dam doesn't look like it's doing anything, but let there be a crack in the dam and we soon discover that holding back allows us to pour forth with more energy. Life is not going to be any more in our control if we are holding it tightly. Sometimes holding something too tightly just lets what's important slip between our fingers.

Hold your children too tightly and, one day, the tension will teach you to let go.

Relaxing is a reminder that passivity need not be a passive state, and being uptight does not necessarily mean that our character is upright.

———•——

People who are relaxed tend to make others feel more comfortable.

Getting other people to relax begins by definition with our loosening up. You can be relaxed and diligent. You can certainly be tense at work and not intensely doing your work.

———•——

Learning to relax is good work. Some people are too lazy to try relaxing.

Those of us who picked up placards in the 1960s are now plugging away at pension plans and beginning to think about picking up fishing poles and fishing for a little peace. A lot of us long ago held up signs that said "Make Peace Not War." Few of us thought about our internal wars or making peace with ourselves.

Some of us live our lives under protest. All of us live our lives under a fair amount of tension. "It's time most of us hung a sign on our attitude: 'Gone Fishing.'"

Only a quiet pond paints an honest picture.

Only an honest person can begin to make peace with his or herself.

11

Finding Direction

Taoist teaching tells us that we should walk down the path of life prepared for the worst evil to jump out and attack us at any moment. We are also told to walk down the path in life and be prepared for the greatest joy to jump out and embrace us. We are further told to walk down the path in life and be prepared for absolutely nothing to happen. AND, we are told to hold all three of these attitudes at the same time.

Life requires us to juggle attitudes. And experience teaches us that altitude is mostly attitude.

What elevates us in life isn't always accessed by an elevator.

But step into a good attitude and you will be amazed at the heights you might reach.

———•———

"If you want to make enemies," said President Woodrow Wilson, "try to change something." We all feel a little weak-kneed at the prospect of moving into unknown terrain or through known fears. On this journey, wisdom is a compass, hope is a lantern, and prayer is a path where there is none.

———•———

Over the millennia, many who have been lost have found their way by finding and following a guiding light.

May we have the compassion to be a light.

May we have the strength to guard the light.

May we have the wisdom to remember that when we're in the spotlight we can seldom see anything.

May we remember that putting the light on ourselves, or keeping others in the dark, is different from being a light or finding and following a light.

———•———

Gifts from the sea, like any gift in life, find their value in our ability to pause and open them. Let us pause to hear poetry in the sound of water rolling rocks in the surf. Let us stop and see broken promises, past lives, and continuity in the pieces of oyster, mussel, and clam shells we find on the beach. Let us have the heart to feel the heat of past passions in the remnants of a brick fireplace eroded into curves and resting on a niche of boulders and driftwood.

Finding our way has much in common with finding the time to appreciate what's directly in front of us.

All of us are heading down the tracks. And while we may not be the engineers of our fate, we are all stationmasters. We can learn to read our interior signals and influence when we leave our "emotional" stations.

Sadness departs and joy arrives on the same set of tracks.

Physicists remind us that what we fix anywhere in the universe fractures something somewhere else. The things we have dealt with will also deal with us.

We can't make a move that doesn't in some way move on us.

Most of us are not lacking for information but for the character to act on what we already know. Most of us are not in a tizzy about how to get where we want to go. The question for most of us is whether we have the character to deal with taking direction.

Where we're going has much to do with how we dealt with where we've been.

A compassionate sage and friend lives at a distance and recently suffered a debilitating stroke. When I called to ask about his condition, I was told he was embracing a meditation of "patience, persistence, and acceptance."

Any of us might find our way by the light of these three candles.

Success isn't always to the swift.

Going slowly can be its own success.

In life, what you catch isn't always what you bait your hook for.

One's life can be a work of art, but it's not always a pretty picture.

Life is not always wonderful, but it is an experience filled with wonder.

The first step to getting in touch with ourself is not to walk away from ourself.

Though we can feel we have lost our way, nothing we have ever done is lost.

Doing is the way we use action to hide the character we are being.

Losing hope, we always lose our way.

Going slowly is sometimes a good way to pick up speed.

Backing up is a good way to pull into spaces where we otherwise might not fit.

It is we who are lost when we don't help others to find their way.

Being where you are is the best way to get wherever you are going.

———

Sometimes stepping back is the best way to get a closer view.

———

Looking at things the way we used to can be a familiar blindness. When you're trying to find your way, watch for your comfortable blindness.

Often the best way to run away from something is to run to something.

Appearances aren't everything in life, though much in life appears that way.

Success is its own gravity. Having more doesn't always help one to soar. Sometimes nothing weighs heavier on us than our success.

"The toughest thing about success," said Irving Berlin, "is that you've got to keep on being a success."

Play the part, not the result. Sometimes the only way to achieve success is not to aim for it. But to feel successful about how we are conducting ourself.

———

Learning isn't prejudiced. Good lessons are not always taught by good people.

Take the best and leave the rest. Don't deny teachers, or yourself, the right to be a person—a person trying to find his or her way.

———

Seeing people heading the wrong way can help us find our way.

Procrastination is always planning a trip and never taking one.

Success is not always sprouted in success. Failure can be a fertilizer.

Growing older is not a magic wand wiping away who we were or are.

No matter our plans for getting anywhere, life has its own freeway system. And the road ahead is always under construction.

Stopping for a moment is sometimes the best way to move forward.

One of the nicest ways to find happiness is to bring a little happiness into the lives of others.

Sometimes the best way to get something done is to give it a rest.

If the truth shall set us free, humility is the best way to begin picking the lock.

Every role we play is a role. There are always new scripts. And always some folks reading old ones. And wanting you in their plays.

——•——

Letting go is not always the same thing as giving up.

Sometimes the sanest way of hanging in is letting go.

——•——

In life there are no one-way streets. Events are coming at us as quickly as we're going anywhere.

Daring to live one's life is the most daring way to live.

Blind faith doesn't mean we're blind.

——•——

The *British Commando Handbook* suggests the following for Army Rangers trying to find their way. For all of us, in or out of the military, the advice has merit:

Listen like a blind man.

Watch like a deaf man.

——•——

12

---◈---

Work and Persistence

Resolutions are promises we make to ourselves. They are a way we draw a line in the sand of our own soul and dare some old habit to cross over.

---◈---

A study of brain physiology teaches us:

To lose a habit, make a new one.

Old habits won't leave until you have new ones to take their place.

To get rid of something negative, do something positive.

---◈---

Our ability to hold to resolutions probably has less value to us than the belief that if we REALLY put our mind to it we can change our behavior. All of us want to think that, at any moment, we could once again be the captain of our own ship.

What's curious about this is that we were the ones who got the captain drunk or locked him in his cabin in the first place, because we didn't want to or were afraid of taking control of our lives.

———◆———

With all respect to genius, perspiration more often than inspiration is the path to day-to-day miracles.

People seldom want a second helping of responsibility.

Resolve is made up of two words that imply that what we can't solve we try to solve again.

———◆———

There is an English proverb that says, "Someday is never." Sometimes that's true. But not just procrastination is at play. Sometimes it just takes time to learn when it is the right time to do anything.

———◆———

A friend of mine is a famous athlete. People are always asking him if this or that piece of exercise equipment really works. "Only if you use them," he answers.

Garages are inevitably filled with exercise equipment. Garages are the elephant graveyards for stationary bikes, rowing machines, and barbells. In garages, we can see earnest resolutions rusting.

Postponed promises and guilt can be stored under drop cloths. These black-plastic mountains also remind many of us of what we had to have and now ignore but cannot throw away.

Every now and then there is a commitment to clean up and straighten up the garage or our life. But, like with exercise, if you lie down for a while the urge passes.

Many of us fall asleep at the helm of our commitments.

————

Procrastination isn't bad by nature, but if others sadden us when they break their promises, we break our own hearts when we put off promises we've made to ourselves.

Some of us write elaborate lists and feel that in writing things down they are done.

Some of us make lists of what we have done or need to get done.

The ego's self-hypnosis says, "Repeat after me: If there is something I must do, I must be important." Lists make us people of consequence even if the acts we're taking note of are completely lacking in consequence.

————

Being busy makes us feel full even when our actions are empty. Being busy is often a distracting camouflage to keep our attention from what we are ignoring.

Lists do not distinguish between "wants" and "needs." They both go on the same list. This gives us an excuse to "need" what we only "want." Our impulses are made legitimate. I crave, therefore I am entitled.

———

We have public lists and private lists, and lists that are private, even to us. Our fears are not afraid to make their own list. Our fears often only let us look at being scared rather than at what scares us.

———

Unlike the list we forget to take to the supermarket, our list of fears never gets left at home. This list certainly influences and usually controls other lists. It's not that we don't do what we're afraid of, it's that we often don't even think of doing what we're afraid of.

Our fears censor our "to do" lists.

———

None of us intend to forget anymore than we want to be forgotten. Lists remind us that we all forget.

———

Even if we get the work we want, it is still work.

Even to fuel passion, you have to chop wood.

———

The dignity of labor is the dignity we bring to our labor. Some of us labor at relationships, alcohol, weight, or self-image.

We ALL have our work even when we can't find work. We ALL have our work even when we're rich enough not to work.

Work rubs us up against ourself. It allows us to see who we are, and the pay is dependent on whether we are paying attention.

———

The Bible says we shall live by the sweat of our brow. And all of us working through the day-to-day have sweated over life. But there is also another angle on this line of scripture. By work we live.

Work gives meaning to life. It isn't always that our work is meaningful but that we find meaning, find ourselves, as a result of work. When we rub up against work, we get a feel for life.

———

Work means we're making something. Making a difference. Making more of life than our problems.

There are people on the planet willing to kill for work and others who feel that their work is killing them.

The linking truth is that work is intimately connected to life. Work is its own music, and the call to work is an eternal muse. Work, like music, can soothe the savage beast. Not listening to what work we should be doing can bring out the beast in us.

———

We can't always be passionate about our work. And sometimes we have to work at our passions. Passion is the stuff of both pain and pleasure. Work, too.

We generally meet people through what they do and are inclined to forget who they may be. Ourselves, too.

Too many of us are in hiding behind our occupations and dying for a little company.

———✦———

The chairman of a company that employs 23,000 people showed me his day care center at corporate headquarters. It was naptime. "This is the one-year-old room," he said as we peeked through the windows. "This is the two-year-old room. This is the three-year-old room." Children curled on mats with blankets and pillows they brought from home. The moms could come at breaks and lunch to connect. Paintings better than mine hung on the walls. The future bodes well for any company that thinks not only of its own future but the future.

———✦———

In the workplace, caring is never misplaced. Caring is always good work.

Worrying about work is often much of the labor in work.

Worrying about whatever we're doing is often much of the labor in whatever we're doing.

———✦———

Rich people need to work. They need to work at making their children understand that inherited wealth doesn't make you a "rich" person.

Work is wealth. Ask someone who can find nothing to do and has all the time to do it.

———•———

Work doesn't have to be fun to make you smile at what you've accomplished.

For some of us our biggest accomplishment is not how much we've made but what we've made of ourselves.

———•———

Take the time to step back from your work. In your efforts, pause to see how you are doing. Afford yourself a Sabbath so you may see that sometimes in the "not doing" much is done.

See how what you do matters even as the little things in life don't seem to matter at all.

A large part of any job is simply paying attention, but paying attention still requires us to pay. And when we don't pay attention, we pay more.

Finding work is not easy. But then, neither is work. Life is a struggle. A wrestling with the intimacies of trying and failing. And trying again. This is life's work.

We're all laboring at who we are. In the social-hive, some of us are "busy-bees," some of us are "wanna-bees," and some of us are worried about what we might no longer be.

———◆———

Parents and teachers often tell kids to think on what they want to be when they grow up. The thought is to help you sort your thoughts and then it is easier to find your way. And it is. But the journey is the way.

Success isn't the arrival but how we travel.

———◆———

Many people who have arrived at successful careers wake up in an airport wondering if they've paid too much for their ticket.

Making plans for where we want to go is ALMOST as important as remembering how we should conduct ourselves along the way.

———◆———

A great deal shouldn't be predicated on us getting more and someone else getting less. A great deal is when the other person is also thinking they got one.

Winning isn't the art of making someone else a loser. That attitude is always a bad deal.

———◆———

The most any of us with vision can hope to see on our journey is our own blindness.

Here are a few reminders:

"Heavier-than-air flying machines are impossible," said Lord Kelvin, President of the Royal Society, in 1895.

"Who the hell wants to hear actors talk?" asked the Founder and CEO of Warner Brothers in 1927.

"I'm just glad it'll be Clark Gable who's falling on his face and not Gary Cooper," said Gary Cooper, deciding not to take the leading role in "Gone With the Wind" in 1937.

"I think there is a world market for maybe five computers," said Thomas Watson, the Chairman of IBM, in 1943.

"We don't like their sound, and guitar music is on the way out," said Decca Recording Co., rejecting the Beatles in 1962.

To quote Yogi Berra, "The future ain't what it used to be."

———•———

If you think you're in the dark remember:

What illuminates a star is the surrounding darkness.

Success is as isolating as it is illuminating.

Anyone trying to find his or her way isn't always going to be hiking at high noon.

Every trail in every life leads through dark moments.

Each of us will have to find our way through our ignorance, and doubt, and despair, and know ourselves as better for the journey.

———•———

"Each of us is in the great darkness of our ignorance. And each of us is on a journey.

In the process of that journey we must bend and build a fire for light, and warmth, and food.

But, when our fingers tear at the ground, hoping to find the coals of another's fire, what we often find are the ashes.

And in these ashes there may be sadness, but there is also testimony.

Because these ashes tell us that somebody else has been in the night, somebody else has bent to build a fire, and somebody else has carried on.

And that can be enough, sometimes."

—Noah benShea, *Jacob the Baker*

———•———

13

---◈---

Community

We need each other not because we think we do, but because we do.

Community by definition means to connect. People who don't connect with each other are not a community.

Let's "lighten up" so that we might be less of a burden to ourselves and a sense of relief to others.

There was a time when a favorite Halloween costume was to dress up like a gangster. Now that's no costume. Violence is commonplace. Perhaps we should put on a smile. And really scare people in our community.

---◈---

The purpose of community is not necessarily what the community votes to be its purpose.

A community's higher purpose is everyone and every one in the community.

———•———

Most of us, most of the time, would rather be distracted than disturbed. This is the premise of the entertainment industry. Music, movies, television serve to keep us distracted. What we share is distraction and the desired avoidance of being disturbed. Consequently much of our shared social sanity is not what we're watching but what we're missing or avoiding, together. Community reminds us that in life we can be alone and together.

Gossip is community conversational pollution. It corrodes community.

———•———

We are all members of one tribe, the tribe of time and vulnerability.

What makes us all blood brothers and sisters is that we all bleed.

All of us have pains. In binding our wounds let us know we are bound together.

———•———

Liking others doesn't mean liking only those who are like us.

We are each the source of the other's river.

Anyone who is filled with himself or herself cannot be increased by others.

When we discover each other's blindness, it is already growing light.

When we offer others a hand, we are lifted.

We can be independent and still dependent on others.

Sometimes it's not until we are around others that we feel alone.

What we can't say to one another is deafening.

What we can't see in one another is blinding.

What we don't know about others isn't their ignorance but ours.

We're all inclined to think that others don't know what we're just learning.

It is we who are lost when we don't help others to find their way.

The moments we share with others remind us we are neighbors in time.

A good sense of humor is when we laugh less at others and more at ourselves.

Anyone who feels good about him- or herself will tend to feel better about others.

People who are comfortable with their own company make the best company.

People who aren't comfortable being alone aren't looking for a relationship, just a way to not be alone.

Often the source of much dishonesty isn't a fear that others will hurt us, but that they won't love us.

Faith by definition does not require proof or need to prove others are wrong.

A community sharing a faith that needs to prove others are wrong isn't sharing its faith but its doubt.

Caring about others is a different concern than caring what others think.

One of the nicest ways to find happiness is to bring a little happiness into the lives of others.

None of us are a gift to others if we're wrapped up in ourselves.

Any of us are taller who stop looking down on others.

Listen to what others are saying to you and to what it says about them.

What you can expect to hear from others are their expectations. Listen for yours.

Often we want others to listen because there is something we need to hear.

No one frees another. Freedom is first a self-declaration.

If you want to sound fascinating, listen to others. Too often communication is an agreement not to listen to each other.

———

Reminding others that they make our life richer enriches us.

———

14

Family

Families are quilts. They are a patchwork of souls. One generation is stitched to the next.

Family is a place where we sometimes give more than we get and often get more than we give.

"If you educate a man you educate a person," said Ruby Manikan, a church leader, "but if you educate a woman you educate a family."

Women help men find their way into family.

In order for fathers to take the lead, they don't always have to be the leader.

Women have helped many men who feared they would never be heroes become heroes to their family.

A man doesn't have to be a hero for his death to be a tragedy.

———————

Husbands and wives often not only accuse each other of being the source of each other's sadness, they'll try to get the other to lug it. Others, however, aren't interested in carrying our sadness. All of us have our own baggage to budge.

Family should be a place where you can set your sadness down.

———————

The people in your life are a bouquet. Wake up and smell the flowers.

———————

First we look up to our parents, then down on them, and finally at them.

———————

"A woman puts her arm in a sweater," said my elderly aunt, "and out comes her mother's hand." At some point, in each of our lives, we begin to observe in our own behavior a trait of our parents. Whether it is a gesture, an inflection, or a habit, these mannerisms and attitudes were handed to us, often without our knowing, and usually carried unopened for years. I call them going-away presents.

The cartoonist and social wit Jules Feiffer was rumored to have quipped, "I grew up to have my father's looks, my father's speech patterns, my father's posture, my father's opinions, and my mother's contempt for my father."

What we get and who we get it from is not always a choice. We can decide to be patient like our mother and discover the anger of our father. We can hope for our father's humor and receive our mother's narrowness. Mix into this confusion the chance that we will get their attitudes on each other and on gender in general, and the pot begins to boil. We have all been served bowls of Parent Soup.

There's an old Yiddish proverb: "When a husband and wife go to bed, there're at least six people in the bed—the husband, the wife, his parents, and hers."

On a secluded beach, I witness a collection of seals using the ocean swells to lift themselves onto a small island of rock. I am struck by how much family is like this piece of real estate.

Family affords us a place to crawl out of the waves. A place to be a child no matter our age. A place where we don't always have to be strong. A place where our weakness may discover its strength.

The tides inevitably rob the seals of the leverage to gain the rock. In all families, too, the tides of time take their toll. But oh, the sweet moment of a family gathered, shoulder to shoulder, warming in the sun.

———•◦•———

We used to say that families were as American as apple pie. And it's true. In families you get a slice of life.

That we belong with others doesn't mean we belong to others.

The people in our life are not our possessions, but we are at a loss when we lose them.

The value of family expands by drawing it closer.

Hold family sacred and what is sacred will hold the family.

The next time we tell our children to "be good," we might remember that they're taking a good hard look at us.

Too often we show our kids the right way to get the wrong things.

Children discover who adults really are by observing what adults want.

Kids know they are vulnerable. Vulnerability is the foundation of fear, and fear is a door to anger. Parents are often targets provided by God so kids can practice projecting their anger.

It was the actor Peter Ustinov who said, "Children sharpen their teeth by chewing on the bones of their parents."

———•———

Parents have more opportunities to read shoulder shrugs than school essays.

Any of us who pays attention can learn what's new from a nuance.

———•———

On the beach, a group of children and their father dig at the sand with small shovels. They are building a castle. The ocean is building a moat. The castles we build in life do not outlast the tides. We know this, we have witnessed this, and yet we invest in our plans.

Children should be encouraged to create castles despite the lurking tides of despair.

We should remind our children and ourselves that sometimes the best way to catch a passion is to slow down and let it catch you.

We should nurture our children's passion. Teach them to tend their inner fire. Fan the flames of their interest and curiosity.

Good parenting requires us to remind our children of their strengths. Life will remind them of their weaknesses. As it has reminded us.

Children raised with love are not weak.

Children raised to be strong often struggle finding the strength to be loving.

If life is like a river, then it's probably a good an idea to teach our children to fish as to worry about how many fish we're going to leave them.

Growing up requires self-parenting.

Parents can't grant us independence and children can't take it.

Independence isn't kept in a drawer and handed over on an appropriate birthday. We're all born free and struggling to earn what we already have.

Parents and children both need to remember that feeling free to be ourselves is a gift we spend a lifetime unwrapping.

First one becomes a man. From there one can aspire to being a father.

Anyone who isn't a good man is going to be a questionable father.

A great deal of being a man and being a father is having the courage, the day-to-day stamina, to be ignored and unappreciated and to carry on.

To be number-one fathers, dads need to remember they don't always come first.

Being a father is a willingness to shoulder a load in life without expecting to get a tie for your efforts on the third Sunday in June.

It's a fact. The most collect phone calls are made on Father's Day.

When men finally get a grip on fatherhood, they are reminded to let go. Not not care. But let go.

Every father should remember that any emotion he is feeling, while entirely his own, is also owned by other men.

Freud threw up his hands over understanding the opposite sex. The final question he asked was, "What do women want?" And while mothers rightly feel they are never understood, fathers consistently feel they are misunderstood. Herein is the brotherhood of men.

Feelings for fathers usually find work in the lost and found. By the time we find out how much we love our dad, we've lost the moment with him.

———•◦•———

It was Jacqueline Kennedy Onassis who said, "If you bungle raising your children, I don't think whatever else you do well matters very much."

With parenting, either you pay now or you pay later. Parents never stop paying. Love always has a cost of admission.

———•◦•———

Mothers can read their children like a book, and when they are bad quote them chapter and verse.

With rare exceptions, moms are gems as rare as they are common.

Like common sense, moms aren't that common.

Mothers learn early that you do not love out of the expectation of being loved back. Children take a mother's love and call when they get a chance. A mother's strength is her ability to love without expectation.

Mothers eventually learn to hug their children by letting go. Mothers who don't learn this, learn why they should.

———•◦•———

"One is not born a woman, one becomes one," noted Simone de Beauvoir in her writings. Mothers, however, are born. They are born in the laps of good mothers. Moms make moms.

Women can become great moms without good mothers, but the becoming requires much overcoming.

———————

Moms teach. Moms run charm schools and boot camps and are often the product of both.

Daughters are moms in training.

Daughters practice by trying to train their moms.

———————

Daughters and moms share sacred passions, but passions shout as often as they whisper.

Moms remind their daughters that life requires both femininity and strength.

Moms remind sons to love women with both these strengths.

Moms remind us that it's okay to be weak, and to show mercy is no weakness.

What makes a mom super is not that she doesn't break down, but how often she gets up.

Mothers aren't always right, but certainly they are here so we are less often wrong.

———————

The struggle of single moms is the stuff of heroes. And though some of these heroes are tragic, what makes a woman a hero is not her fall but her courage in getting up.

Single moms don't have a lot of airtime. They talk when someone will listen. They talk to themselves and each other. They talk above the white noise of tantrums, reminding, and sniffling. You can, I discovered, wipe a child's nose and tell a friend you're climbing the walls in the same swipe.

Single moms feel like they're standing on the edge of a huge precipice shouting with less expectation of being heard than of having the company of their own echo.

———

What makes single dads men of steel is not that they don't feel, but that they keep on going when they feel too much.

When parents split up, dads shouldn't split.

Dads who don't live with their kids don't stop being fathers. Being a dad isn't something you can step back too far from without stepping off the cliff.

Dads can leave, but they can't leave their responsibility.

Every father isn't an angel, but they have the capacity. Dads who don't flee from being dad fly the highest.

———

My father was a man of much love and few words. When we rode together in a car, we would sit next to each other for hours, and he would say almost nothing. In that quiet we shared, I felt his deepest presence. Several years back I noticed I had been driving with my son for a prolonged period and had said nothing. I am not a man of few words, and I heard my father in that journey of silence.

Fathers and sons share a silent bond. Much that is meaningful in life runs silent and deep.

"How was school?" was the first question my father asked when he came home. I would answer, "Okay." "What didya learn?" was always his second question. "Nothin' special," was always my second answer. He wasn't really asking. I wasn't really answering. But we were talking. He was telling me he was thinking about me. I was telling him I could hear him caring.

Caring is connecting. My father died over a decade ago, and we're still connected. I tell people that my dad died; he's not gone. Or, to borrow a reversal from all the Elvis sightings, my dad may have left the room but not the building.

Fathers and sons have to stay on the line even when the other end goes silent.

⸻ ⬦ ⸻

Listening to your kids doesn't just mean listening to what they say, but to what they don't say. Almost all real listening, but parental listening for sure, requires listening to the silences.

My daughter, as a child, would climb into my lap, and I was hers. Even when I thought I was inflexible, she made me a yogi. She could bend me any way she wanted. With a pouting lip, daughters turn dads inside out, and fathers find there is value in being vulnerable.

Perfect parents, like perfect love, is a contradiction in terms.

⸻ ⬦ ⸻

Teenage daughters are not only trying on clothes. They are also trying on emotions. And all things considered, no matter where they're going emotionally they'd rather ride a roller-coaster than a bus. More often than not I'd be busy reacting to my daughter's last feelings when she was already trying on new ones. More often than not I'd be busy reacting to her feelings when she was only taking her feelings out for a spin to see, well . . . how they feel. It took me a while and a few more bruised moments to catch this spin. But I did. Even took a few rides with her.

———

Parenting isn't anything if it isn't a study in patience. I've lost my patience often with my daughter. Sometimes she's helped me find it.

Daughters help dads find feelings they never knew were lost.

———

Dads certainly don't need to be good looking, but do sometimes need to look the other way.

———

Parenting is a process of moving from management to consultant, if you're lucky.

Do not kiss your children so they will kiss you back, but so they will kiss their children and their children's children.

———

15

—◦◦◦—

Paying Attention

In the long run, paying attention is usually wiser than being the subject of attention.

It isn't always the Big Bad Wolf that has to be dealt with. Small, unattended annoyances are also at large. It may be that "little things worry little minds," as the American proverb reminds us, but the little things in life are also worth the attention of large minds.

Watch what causes your ripples. Watch where your ripples find shore. Pay attention to your pond.

—◦◦—

I know nothing about wallpaper except that in some social situations I've felt like wallpaper, with ears. Ignored and listening, one can learn much.

Sometimes what we're dying to see is right under our nose, and we can't see it because we've been looking so hard for it.

———•———

The obvious is often hidden in its obviousness.

People who remind others or heal others of their blindness can be people walking around with blinders.

What we don't want to see often gets overlooked.

———•———

A friend of mine called recently to talk about his relationship with a woman he had been seeing for a number of years. "The problem," he said, "is that there are some things about her that have long bothered me, and I've never said anything. There's been an elephant in the living room of our relationship and we've been denying it."

"My friend," I replied, "the elephants are everywhere."

———•———

For many of us, personally and professionally, there is an elephant in the living room, or the bedroom, or the boardroom that we ignore, deny, or simply walk around as if it were not there. When we shut our eyes, the world does not go into hiding.

Even if we have a nose for news, it's sometimes the thing right under our nose that we miss. Often what we miss is what we'd just as soon miss. Can you imagine that?

Even when we've been repeatedly stepped on by the elephant—even when we've had to pick up a shovel and shovel up the mess the elephant left behind—we often refuse to pay attention to the pachyderm. Ladies and gentlemen, an elephant is an elephant. Telling ourselves that it's a big gray mouse and being politically correct about this mouse's unusually large nose doesn't serve us or the elephant and every elephant is not a kindly Dumbo. We often don't miss the elephants in our life because they're hiding under the carpet.

Fool me once, shame on you; fool me twice, shame on me. What was missed wasn't missed, because it was missing—after all, we are talking about an elephant. People who like to think they are insightful can still be shortsighted.

People today are aware of more and know less than any previous generation. We are awash in information but suffering a drought of experience. Almost every kid knows where milk comes from, but almost none of them have milked a cow.

Knowing something is very different from knowing about something. Paying attention is never something that can be put on a pay-later plan without having to pay more.

Learning is learning that much of what we know was known before us.

Humility is the door to every schoolhouse.

Paying attention means noting when we're not paying attention.

In order for a house to be a house it must have a window and a door.

A door so we can come into our self.

And a window so we can see beyond our self.

———•———

Life is an experience at sea. Learning comes in waves. Pay attention to the waves. Even as they threaten to swamp you.

Focus brings not only the world but also us into focus.

———•———

Let's pay attention not only to who's important, but also to what's important.

Let's pay attention not only to what's important, but also what it does to whom.

If we don't pay attention, we pay later.

———•———

The future pays for the past, and pays the most when we haven't paid attention.

In life there are fewer surprises than lapses of attention.

Acceptance can sometimes be the nicest way of giving others attention.

The "pay" in paying attention isn't the cost for paying attention but for not paying attention. Little costs more than not paying attention.

———————

Look with your heart. Caring is a corrective lens.

Wisdom surrounds us. It is seldom hidden, but is often overlooked.

———————

Looking at life and seeing little of value can be very expensive.

What we won't look at is our chosen blindness.

Once we sort people by what they do, we look at them without seeing who they are.

———————

If you're looking for romance in your life, begin with having a heart-to-heart with yourself.

Looking away is too often our way of looking.

If you're looking for a second chance, take a second look.

———————

Often when we're looking out for what can go wrong, we've got to look in, not out.

Desire fuels desire. Getting what we want doesn't keep us from wanting.

No matter what we're looking at, what we're seeing is our mind.

Every epiphany does not require an exceptional moment and often requires only a person prepared to pay attention to the exceptional.

A miracle is often our willingness to see the common in an uncommon way.

———•·•———

Too many of us feel that in order to pay attention our mind has to be standing at attention. At ease, soldier. Sometimes the best way to take a hard look at things is to relax. Tension is not the same as paying attention.

Life tests all of us. Pay attention. And take notes.

———•·•———

16

Spirituality and
Inspiration

Prayer is a path where there is none.

The reason for religion is not reason.

Pray less "please" and more "thank you."

Life is a gift. Prayer is a thank-you note.

Staying in touch with our own soul is a good way to remember that souls aren't lost except as we lose touch.

Our soul affords us harbor, but every soul sooner or later finds itself in rough water. Souls that do not drown are made stronger by the seas they swim through. Every soul needs a light to swim toward. A sighting. And spiritual insight can be that sighting.

It used to be that when we reached a moral crossroads we would say, "I've got to do some soul searching." It didn't mean we set out to find our soul. It meant we had to examine our soul. See how we felt. See who we were. Envision who we would become if we turned left instead of right.

In soul searching, the "searching" is its own victory. Soul searching is not something one does with the hope of becoming more, but better.

———•◦•———

In the work of soul searching there is no time off, just as life affords no time outs.

Soul work is as tiring as it is exhilarating.

Taking stock of one's self seldom pays in publicly traded stock, but it is money in the bank. Soul work affords us resources that we can later draw on. Most of us forget this until our spirits are overdrawn.

When we as "soul-keepers" misinterpret our duty as a commitment to drudgery, we have incarcerated the soul.

The purpose of a higher purpose is to elevate. We guard our soul to ensure its altitude and not to drag it down with our attitude of rectitude.

———•◦•———

Laughter can be an act of piety.

God smiled on us in the hope that we would smile back.

———•◦•———

We sanctify the future when we remember the souls who have passed.

We transform our lives by taking the time to examine a passing moment's soul.

St. Augustine said, "Faith is to believe what you do not see; the reward for this faith is to see what you believe." Faith doesn't think it's right. It has faith that it's right. The human spirit is triumphant because it has faith in the possible. Believe in what is possible. What is impossible will come to its own end.

Babe Ruth struck out almost twice as many times as he hit a home run. And he was the best of the best. Keep swinging, that's the lesson. For all of us. At least that's the attitude to take to the game. Life is about taking the field and taking our swings.

Faith is not news. But it is always new to the predicament. Biblical commentary explains that the Red Sea did not part because Moses raised his staff, but because one Israelite threw himself into the waters with the faith he would not drown.

The path ahead of us is often less a rocky road of reason than a leap of faith.

Our emotions have seasons. Faith is our capacity to weather our own doubt.

The lesson of faith is more than the faith that "there will be enough." It is rather the faith that we will yet learn what is enough.

Faith's challenge is not to believe that we will get more, but become more.

Life is not in our control, but that does not mean it is out of control.

———•••———

We cannot control what happens to us. We can control how we respond to what happens to us.

Faith sees beyond fate.

Faith is trust finding its way in the dark.

———•••———

Faith is the consummate night-light. Leave yours on.

———•••———

Prayer not only changes things but the people praying. Prayer reminds us that we matter, we make a difference, we can change things. We might want to pray that we don't forget this.

When I'm in the middle of prayer, I'm not thinking about what religion the person next to me is or isn't. That's something that happens when I fall out of prayer.

Prayer reminds us that there are higher character issues than finding fault with others—issues like looking at our own faults.

———•••———

Through a forest of hurt, prayer is a path.

All our prayers are not answered, but all prayers are heard. If only by the person praying.

———————

Hope is prayer's balm.

If you think this is foolish, what is the wisdom of despair?

———————

A recent survey of almost 100,000 patients found that those who attended church at least once a week had half the heart disease of those who didn't. Even when prayer does not heal, it helps.

Prayer is a physician to pain.

———————

Little lifts spirits like being in good spirits.

Broken plans don't have to break our spirit.

———————

George Bernard Shaw said, "In heaven an angel is nobody in particular." And he was right. Any of us looking for a set of wings can always carve a pair from humility, but never from pride.

I've seen angels a number of times. They have always been in human form, and I have never known they were angels when I met them. Let us not hide that part in any of us that is angelic.

In order to see an angel, be an angel.

That we don't know the purpose of angels doesn't mean they are without purpose. Angels are messengers of a higher purpose than our own.

———•◦•———

Angels aren't maids. Angels don't do windows. Angels get their agenda from another altitude. We have to clean our own windows if we would hope to see angels.

Sometimes we're angels to others and don't know it. Sometimes that's what makes us angels.

———•◦•———

Angels remind us of our capacity to be angels to ourselves.

The acts of angels are not always obvious. Indeed, the actions of angels may not at all be visible in the present tense. That we do not see the Hand of God speaks only of our blindness. To be a person of vision first requires us to see our blindness.

Angels seem to have seasons. We are more inclined to see angels around religious holidays. This probably has less to do with angels and more to do with when we are paying attention—or when we leave the door to our soul unlocked.

Seeing with our heart is a good way to keep an eye out for angels.

Be loving and others will see the angel in you.

Voltaire said, "If God created us in His own image we have more than reciprocated." Unfortunately, too many of us confuse looking for God with looking in the mirror. Too many of us want others to treat us as if we were a gift from heaven. And we are. What we forget is that we all are.

———

False gods tell us less than they say about us. And what they say about us is that we desperately want something to believe in.

False gods feed on fears. And we see that they are well fed.

———

Putting others on a pedestal doesn't make them God. People who climb down from their pedestals should be held in high regard. Even Moses had to come down the mountain.

———

These days, false gods don't go by names we know from the Bible. If they did, it would be easy to know one when we set up an altar.

False gods aren't going to go away. We need them because we feel we do, and salesmen arrive as opportunity provides.

We are all looking for something to be the object of our hope. But being rich, or famous, or thin does not make us gods any more than being poor, anonymous, or overweight means we have not been made in God's image.

False gods are dead ends and not, as advertised, the highway to heaven. That staircase is our soul.

————•————

When we are inspiring, we find ourselves inspired. To inspire others means, by definition, to fill them with our breath. We can breathe life into others but need to remember that all breath is borrowed. Each breath we take must be released. Each life is on loan.

————•————

Inspiration can speak to those who speak well, as well as to those who feel they have nothing to say.

Inspiration reminds us that even if our lives are sad stories, we can still write a happy ending. A blind man recently wrote a book by picking out letters by blinking. Researchers say we all blink once every five seconds. This means 300 times an hour, 7,200 times a day; 2,628,000 times a year each of us is blind. Out of this blindness some of us fashion excuses and some of us write books by blinking signals to a computer. Inspiration is an equal opportunity employer.

Many of us have the right to be excused from the expectation of others, but all of us should expect great things from ourselves.

Inspiration can breathe life into our courage. Be self-inspiring. Resuscitate yourself.

People who are dis-spirited are dis-heartened.

Have a heart and you will find your spirit.

One of the words for soul in Hebrew is also the word for wind because it was the breath of God that blew life into the clay and made life. When I feel the wind, I can feel God breathing. And feel more alive. Watch the trees in the wind and see the world's chest rising and falling. And rising.

Many of us are afraid to address our spirituality. Many of us feel we can talk to clerics and leave it to them to talk with God. I've never been in any cleric's office and seen the "red phone." Drop a dime. Make a call. Operators are waiting.

17

---◆---

Humor

Humor teaches tolerance," said W. Somerset Maugham. And he's right. But, perhaps he has it backward. Perhaps tolerance and acceptance, certainly of ourselves, teaches us to have a sense of humor.

People who can't laugh at themselves are those who most often laugh at others.

Money and power leave their mark, but people who make us laugh leave a hole when they leave.

---◆---

Too many of us think that in order to be taken seriously, the first thing we have to do is lose our sense of humor.

How could anyone take us seriously if we couldn't laugh at ourselves? How could we?

Sometimes we are all full of hot air. Poking fun at ourselves can be the perfect pin.

It's funny what people find funny. Victim humor isn't funny if you're the victim.

People also use humor to hate, but humor isn't an excuse to make someone else hurt.

Humor's great gift is the release it affords us when we're hurting.

When life seems a little chilly, remember humor warms the heart.

Throw a log on your fire.

Laughing lightens our load. It helps us lighten-up.

Laughing at life's circumstances is an act of courage. It is contempt with grace. It is good style when the only thing you can afford is a good attitude.

Against the darkness, laughter is a lantern.

Humor is not a long-winded argument. The truth may set us free, but if it does it with a laugh, we're more inclined to take notes.

Laughing at those in power gives us power over them.

Once we've decided to smile, our smile helps us decide a lot of other things.

Laughing at ourselves is a wake-up call. It helps us wake up with a smile on our face.

Of all the things we can have, why not have a laugh?

———◆———

A husband opened the bottom drawer of his wife's bureau and lifted out a tissue-wrapped package. He discarded the tissue. The slip was exquisite; silk, handmade, and trimmed with a cobweb of lace. The price tag with an astronomical figure on it was still attached. The husband remembered that he bought this the first time they went to New York on a vacation. She never wore it. She was saving it for a special occasion. "Well," thought the husband, "I guess this is the occasion."

Then he took the slip and put it on the bed with the other clothes he was taking to the mortician. His hands lingered on the soft material for a moment, and then he slammed the drawer shut.

Life doesn't always leave us laughing. Sometimes the people we love the most leave and leave us crying.

———◆———

Life is short. And then you die. Forget about whatever is making you crazy today. There will be new things making you crazy tomorrow. Or the day after. It's crazy to spend your days thinking about what's going to make you crazy.

Eating healthy food doesn't necessarily make you a healthy person. Hitler was a vegetarian. Sometimes being sensible just doesn't make sense. People who are always right are usually wrong. There are some situations when it isn't right to laugh, but more often than not nothing will set us right like laughing.

"Fishing for a good time," sings Tom Waits, "starts with throwing in your line." Some of us are so busy fishing for success or happiness we forget what real success is or what makes us happy.

Make happiness your ice cream parlor. Two scoops, please.

We're all breast-fed on social success notions, but it was Lincoln who reminded us, "Most folks are as happy as they make up their minds to be." By the time we grow up we often forget how easy it is to make ourselves happy. "If you really want to be happy," said Sister Mary Tricky, echoing Lincoln, "nobody can stop you." Perhaps now is a good time to stop being your sense of humor's traffic cop. Give yourself the green light to laugh.

Forget about guilt. Guilt, a friend likes to remind me, is somebody else's emotion. Forget about it.

Most people don't do things to us, they do things for them.

Take a few moments you think are spare change and change. Change who you are or what or who you're blaming for why you're not making changes that will make you happy. If this fails, here's a modest proposal. Blame someone else. Make a list of all the people you want to blame for everything that didn't work out the way you wanted in your life. Keep the list handy. When people ask you why you're looking a little blue, pull out the blame list and point to a name. Any name will do, but moms or dads are generally very convenient to put at the head of the list. And, besides, moms and dads often have their moms and dads at the head of their list.

Just to prove that the wives of Presidents could be as sage as their husbands, here's what Martha Washington had to say: "The greater part of our happiness or misery depends on our dispositions, and not on our circumstances." Our happiness or our sadness is not an independent state. It is often dependent on us.

If you want to leave your kids something, leave them a picture of you smiling.

Doing something silly isn't silly. Anymore than being serious about something necessarily makes it serious stuff.

People who are stuck on themselves get stuck in themselves. There is no quicksand like ego.

Give yourself some smiling room because too soon we're all taken away to make more room.

Laughing is sometimes the best way to cry.

When my father was in the hospital suffering from a terminal illness, I would try to be fully with him in that moment. When I left the hospital and returned home, my children would run to hug me, and wanted me to play with them, and wanted me to laugh with them. And I needed to be fully in that moment. And until then it had never dawned on me how much courage it takes to be fully with our sadness, and fully with our laughter, and to be fully in each moment because the next moment is promised to no one. Sometimes happiness is courage smiling bravely.

Fight back the urge to stifle your own laughter. Remember that when we were kids the worst embarrassment was being picked last for a team, war was a card game, and water balloons were the ultimate weapon. Buy a bag of balloons, fill them with water, and see how high you can throw them until they break when you try to catch them. Fill them with watercolor paint and challenge your kids to a backyard contest. First one to turn blue loses.

I'd like you to stop and think for a moment about what was the most ridiculous thing you ever did that others do or don't know about. Now tell me, when you think back on this event, isn't it one of the moments in your life you most treasure? And tell me if one day, when maybe your grandkids are sitting next to you and you want to share a laugh, won't they get a kick out of hearing that story. For sure, you will.

I was recently walking with a friend and found myself reliving out loud a painful memory. After I had gone on for about twenty minutes, my friend asked, "Do you have any idea how much laugh-time you just gave away?"

Life isn't always a laughing matter, and that's what makes laughing such an important matter.

Years ago, and more than a few years ago it was, when people listened to small records called "45s," each record had what was called an "A" side and a "B" side. The sides were called that so disc jockeys knew what side to play on the air. The "A" side was the recording that the record's producer thought had the best chance of being a hit. But sometimes, however, the hit was on the flip side. Sometimes in life the hit is also on the flip side. Often what we think will be the hit in our life doesn't turn out to be the song we find ourselves humming. Life does have an "A" side and a "B" side, although sometimes the difference is a matter of perspective and time. Often in life, people who suffer the most survive out of their ability to turn hurt into humor. The ability to laugh at ourselves is its own healing.

This is not to say that life is always funny or we should laugh at every sadness. It is to say that even when life is served on a golden platter, it is served with an "A" side and a "B" side. And just like the old 45s, the world revolves on this truth. Some days are bigger hits than others. Some days the blue-plate special is the blues. Some days the soup du jour is finding ourselves in the soup.

Life is short. And often tearful. When you're feeling sad, try the flip side. Find a melody in your melancholy.

Because I'm a guy who almost always sings off tune, I don't sing for anyone else's pleasure. Indeed, it sometimes pleasures people for me to stop singing.

I sing so badly that when I sing the national anthem at ball games people think I'm making a political statement.

Small minds are upset by small things.

File this under Self-Esteem. A pussycat staring in a mirror sees a lion. The lesson? Little roars for our attention like our ego. And little can eat us alive like our ego. Tame your humor by learning to laugh at yourself.

———— ·•·•· ————

During the Holocaust, the caring and sage Rabbi Leo Baeck of Berlin, rather than fleeing, went with his parishioners into a German concentration camp. And survived. Asked, years later, what his job was in the camp, he said, "I was a horse."

"A horse?"

"Yes," he said, "I was put in a harness and pulled a wagon filled with the dead."

"How did you emotionally survive?"

"Well," said Baeck, "there was another 'horse' strapped next to me. And he was a philosopher. And we could talk."

———•———

Don't give up your laugh-time. Put more laugh-time in your lifetime. My singing may not make others smile, but it does make them laugh. That we can't always find something to laugh about only makes laughter all the more important.

———•———

Time and laughter is the best way to suture old wounds.

Parenting is no laughing matter, so don't lose your sense of humor or you'll lose your way with your children.

Having a good laugh at our fears is sometimes the only way to dry our tears.

If you want to leave your kids something, leave them laughing.

———•———

Sadness can be a smile that just hasn't turned the next corner.

Laughter is the best umbrella to hold up when sadness showers us.

———•———

18

—⊰•◆•⊱—

Diversity

Y ou matter. Knowing that allows you to embrace that others also matter.

Hold to you and what you hold true, and truly you will feel hugged. Hug what is different in you and the differences in others will not repel you.

Treasure your own company, and you will value the world.

—⊰•◆•⊱—

Life's weather weathers us. Sometimes we storm against ourselves, and on other occasions weathering ourselves is its own trial.

What often makes for bad emotional weather is a worry over what others will think. It isn't that we expect too much of ourselves as much as we worry about the expectations of others. All expectation is eventually wed to disappointment.

———•—•———

Okay. Here's the scene. It's the stuff of Cecil B. DeMille. Flash back 3,500 years. Desert. Mountains. Hot sun. Several hundred thousand people in sheets and sandals. The High Priest lifts a goat over his head and confesses all the sins of the people. The crowd roars. The goat is chased into the wilderness. People throw rocks at it. The crowd roars, again. Everyone feels better—for a while.

Anything that takes the heat off of us for a while makes us feel better for a while. The idea of blaming someone else and driving them away in the hopes that we will feel better is as old as the hills. Those hills remain. We can see them from our windows. Any window in any town. Scapegoats are always in season.

———•—•———

The term *scapegoat* is welded together from the word "escape" and the Hebrew word *aza-zel,* goat, for Azazel, a demon of the desert. Literally, then, the scapegoat functions to liberate our demons. The act of driving off the scapegoat serves to liberate us from our demons, and for most of us our demons are our fears about the consequence of our actions. Guilt, say psychologists, is something we feel about what we've done. Shame, they say, is how we feel others feel about what we've done.

Scapegoats are deluxe escape clauses. They have two horns. Honk once if you feel guilty. Twice if you feel shame. All of us, at one time or another, have played "Get the Goat." None of us elude responsibility by attempting to chase it away.

The scapegoat is always an "other." As soon as we make someone an "other" we no longer have to worry about them resembling us—and don't have to think about how we would feel if this was happening to us. De-humanizing someone makes our crime for de-humanizing them less of a problem to our sense of self—our shared humanity.

In the late Al Capp's *Li'l Abner* comic strip there were pillowy little characters called "Shmoos." They existed solely so everyone had something to kick. The Shmoo relieved pressure. Made everyone feel better. For a while. And when folks felt badly again, as they inevitably did for dealing with the pain not the problem, well, they would, again, give some Shmoo the boot. Ahhhh.

To fire up my old motorcycle I used to have to "kick start" it. Sometimes people need that, too. Sometimes when we have the urge to kick someone else, it's ourselves we need to kick in the rear. Life sneaks up on all of us. Just when we think we're looking at life dead-on we discover we're dead wrong. Life kicks all of us in the can. Sometimes just to wake us up. Sometimes just to move us farther down the trail. And sometimes just because it can. All of us kick around who we can blame instead of looking at ourselves and correcting our aim.

It's tough to drive a scapegoat into the desert when you're under water. Scapegoats were the only animals Noah didn't take aboard the ark. Noah wasn't looking for excuses. The people who always had excuses for how they treated others were the ones left treading water—for forty days and forty nights.

People who are pressured are almost always the midwives of scapegoats. Blame is often born out of what we can no longer bear. Or don't want to. In the movie *Donnie Brasco,* Al Pacino plays a small-time hood named "Lefty" who is on the way to getting "whacked." Lefty knows destiny is packing a piece and tapping its toe just around the corner. He tells the guy driving the car to "stop riding the brake." Then Pacino, with eyes sad as truth, tells the driver, "I'm a spoke, a spoke in a wheel. And so are you."

Don't make your pain turn you into a source of pain to others.

Sometimes in life you can't buy a scapegoat. Sometimes in life we're the goat. And deserve to be. We're all somebody else's excuse or use somebody else for our excuse. And none of us is excused for doing this. We're all on the wheel. Destiny doesn't ride the brake. Discrimination doesn't discriminate. Discrimination has an equal age, race, religion, and gender bias.

The social cartoonist Jules Feiffer had a series of drawings he did once where the captions read: "First they came for the Jews, and I did nothing. Then they came for the Catholics, and I did nothing. Then they came for the Trade Unionists, and I did nothing. And then they came for me, and there was no one left to do anything."

The flag of India is a wheel. The spokes represent the varying aspects of the country and culture. At the time of the country's creation, Prime Minister Jawaharlal Nehru reminded Britain's Lord Mountbatten that there were more than 500 principalities being wrapped up into the new state. To be a spoke in the Indian wheel means to be part of something larger, a part that makes the whole work, makes the wheel turn.

———•·•———

"Others" are always the best species of scapegoat.

White people, black people, people of color, people of other color, other sex, tall people, short people, Jews, Christians, Muslims, surfers, bikers, freaks, straights, redheads, blondes, left-wingers, right-wingers, Commies, members of the Loyal Order of Elks, and more folks than you can throw a stick at have all been scapegoats and had sticks and stones thrown at them. The irony is that no matter how hard we chase others we're usually chasing our own tail. Most of us who want to rid ourselves of our demons should stand in front of a mirror and say, "Baaaa."

———

Don't get me wrong. I know scapegoats play a valuable role in the expiation of guilt and sin. "To deny all is to confess all," says a Spanish proverb, and while all of us have to pay penance, there is little reason why we have to pay more. Or make others pay for us. But when I visit the workplace, the living room, or the bedroom, I often see folks with a scapegoat tethered to a desk, a lamp, or a bedpost.

Most of us like to keep a scapegoat at hand. You never know when you might need one. Scapegoats are like flashlights. They are helpful when things look dark. Unlike flashlights, scapegoats don't always help us find our way. More often they tell us that we've lost our way. Be cautious of a prophet walking with his scapegoat.

The history of scapegoats is the history of sadness. Crowds are often a collection of individuals feeling crowded. People who seek power have long learned that there is little a crowd, or an individual, likes more than avoiding responsibility. If you want to feed a crowd, throw a scapegoat on the "barbie," as they say in Australia.

Down under or up here, the public menu is poorly served when it is served scapegoat. Eating others may be a modest proposal, to borrow from Jonathan Swift, but it's only modest because it's us proposing. Those who engage in "scapegoating" because God tells them to are wed to the Devil. And then, things heat up for everyone.

———

Hate is its own heat. In a cold world, hate is like burning down our house so we can stand there and warm our hands.

Most of us will buy whatever we think will make us feel better. Fewer of us will change whatever we're doing that makes us feel badly. Scapegoats are a historic purchase. But scapegoats don't buy us peace. They buy us time. A little time. And maybe it's about time that we stopped blaming others. Time isn't running out. But it is running. And God has a stopwatch on all of us.

———

In the mid-1970s, I found myself at a tea party with the late visionary philosopher and engineer Buckminster Fuller. He and I were on a faculty together and this was our first, and last, meeting. He was a short man with short hair and thick glasses who would inform audiences that he could tell them everything he knew in just under sixty hours. Struck to be in his company, and still trying to find my own path, I asked him how he found his. "Oh," he said, pushing the bridge of his glasses back on his nose, "when I was much younger I kept trying to fit in and people kept pushing me away. They kept telling me I just didn't fit in. Soon, so many people kept pushing me away, I found I had a perspective." He looked at me like an aged boy and smiled.

———

Fuller found his fit by not fitting. Herein was wisdom.

Most of us spend our lives trying to find where we fit in and feeling saddened by where we don't fit.

Time teaches us that not fitting in can cut in our favor.

Others, who tell us we don't fit in, can actually be doing us a favor.

One fall Friday, a long time ago, a college friend made a mad dash to the airport for a flight to the Middle East. He arrived only to find that his reserved seat had been given to a woman at the last minute. My friend argued and then screamed that this wasn't right, that this was his seat, that they must be able to fit him on this flight. But it was to no avail. The flight went off without him. The woman who took his seat hijacked the plane.

———

Fate and where we fit often cross paths.

Fate can be God's way of showing us how we fit and don't.

Where we fit in life has nothing to do with whether we're fit.

———

When I was growing up, my family moved a great deal. I was constantly changing schools. I wanted to fit in, but as every social group had its own clothes and codes, I was constantly having to adapt, and I became good at adapting—a little too good for my own good. It wasn't that I wanted to be disingenuous, I just wanted to have friends, and I was amazed at my capacity to trade self for company. A bad trade then and now.

Making friends with ourselves requires us to meet ourselves. Unfortunately this is a meeting that many of us postpone. "Integrity," said Eric Fromm, "simply means a willingness not to violate one's identity."

Acceptance can sometimes be the nicest way of giving others attention.

All self-empowerment begins with self-acceptance. Other-acceptance begins with self-acceptance. People who are still struggling to accept who they are will always have trouble accepting others.

Exceptional people are those who are willing to accept what is exceptional in others.

In embracing our fears, letting ourselves know we accept our fears, we become courageous. And from this place, we can do anything.

There is old wine in new bottles and new wine in old bottles. When you're picking a wine, make sure you're picking the wine and not the bottle.

"How unhappy is he who cannot forgive himself," asked Publilius Syrus more than two thousand years ago. Well, I'll tell you, Publilius, unhappy enough to always find something to be angry about in others.

Greatness is not always what you reach but what you reach for. In the Bible it is written that "justice, justice, shall you pursue." It is the pursuit of justice that is noble. "Pursue justice but love mercy," says scripture. It is the reaching out to others that is caring. Justice and caring are goals we are no less for not reaching, but much less for not chasing.

The opposite of love is not hate. The opposite of love is indifference. To be indifferent to the fate of others is to live outside the passions of love and hate. A society that is indifferent to others is uncaring. A society that is indifferent is, by definition, neither passionate nor compassionate.

Rather than personalize our disregard, we often institutionalize our indifference. The social institutionalization of indifference is the insidious and odious opposite of social loving. We may wonder if we have resources, feelings, or fiscal to do the right thing, but by staying out of things we are certainly subsidizing the status quo. And it is time to say, whoa! "History never repeats itself," said Voltaire, "man always does."

Certainly one of the ways that "man" repeats himself and history records it is in a rush to judgment. Our brain physiology requires us to know what goes where. The actual physical makeup of our brain demands that we sort what we know and usually sort it in ways that we used to know or sort of know. What our brain is repelled by is not sorting. Diversity challenges us physiologically, so either we make up our mind or our mind will make us.

We are all fragile. Any of us can be broken. Some of us already spend our days trying to put together the pieces.

———•◦•———

To know ourselves at our highest is to emulate the qualities of the Divine. God is all-powerful, all knowing, all loving. When we pray, we often call out for strength and insight. We more seldom pray to be loving. We emulate God's judgment, but forget that divine justice is divine because God is also loving.

Too many of us have judgment for all and mercy for none.

All of us have feelings. Some of us forget to feel for others.

When a man asks a woman to marry him, he often gives her a diamond ring. It's worth remembering that even the most beautiful diamonds have flaws. The Talmud says, "Great men, great flaws." And the same is true of great women. A willingness to love his and/or her flaws is what makes for a great relationship.

———

Every diamond begins as a lump of coal. A willingness to work on our own flaws is what can make any of us a diamond.

———

"For with what judgment ye judge," says Matthew 7:2, "ye shall be judged." Respect is reciprocal. So is prejudice, unfortunately.

We all hope that mercy is the view from heaven. Heaven help us if we don't return the look.

Let us celebrate our differences instead of our indifference.

A giant is anyone able to see past his or her own opinion.

We all have different beliefs but all have believing and a need to believe in common.

Making someone less does not make us more.

———

19

———⊰•◆•⊱———

Money

No teacher or administrator ever has to apologize for asking for money for education. If the community offered, the request would never have to be made.

Either the key to your wallet is in your heart or the key to your heart is in your wallet.

Think in terms of economics. Anything we can learn is a gift, considering the cost of ignorance. Anything we can come to appreciate in others reduces our self-depreciation.

The basic rule of money is that the cost of having your money anywhere is what it might be earning somewhere else. My theory on the economics of self is as follows: The cost of being who we are at any moment is measured against who we might be.

"Enough" is drawn from the ancient Anglo Saxon, meaning: It suffices. Enough is a critical-mass issue. Like reality, enough is measured by what is not enough and what is too much.

Making a lot of money is different from living a rich life.

To become rich, we must mine ourselves.

Finding our balance on enough is no less challenging than finding our balance anywhere else.

———•———

Hunger is always the best spice.

We pull "enough" from the oven when we can't wait any longer.

———•———

We seldom feel we have enough when more is available. We stop eating cookies when our mother slaps our hand or our vanity sees itself in the mirror wearing a bathing suit.

Even when we're stuffed, we want more stuff. If our stomach is full we immediately begin searching our desires for other vacancies.

———•———

Often those of us who want for little, want more.

Sometimes the only cure to wanting more is to say, "ENOUGH!"

For many, what really scares us is not a life absent of what we want, but admitting what we want.

Many of us don't want our share of the cookies. We want the cookie jar. Many of us "need" what we want when what we need is to want less.

Feelings of emptiness are not diminished by a house full of stuff. Enough "stuff" is seldom the stuff of happiness.

One person is enough to fill an empty life. Ask someone who feels alone.

A while back I heard a wealthy older woman wail, "With my morning walk, my massage, my luncheon, and my afternoon card game, there's no time left for me."

Having a lot of money is often a form of amnesia. We forget what we really have.

Don't forget to:

Take the time to help those who have less than you.

Take more time to do the same.

Take out some old clothes and take a walk.

Take a hot bath and cool down.

Tell your children your love for them is unqualified.

Tell them again.

Laugh at yourself.

And thank God for your struggle.

Money can make us a fortune but leave us wondering if we're really fortunate.

———•———

"The only thing that money solves," said Johnny Carson, "is money problems."

May we look to what we want in life and be blessed with what we need.

Charity is not a luxury of the rich. "One must be poor," said the writer George Elliot, "to know the luxury of giving."

The stuff of life isn't stuff. The important things in life aren't things. And that's the thing to remember.

We live in a world where we often confuse people's worth with how much they are worth.

We confuse making a good living with living a good life.

We confuse things with things that matter.

We often keep a close eye on the stuff that doesn't matter and are blind to the stuff in life that does matter. Focusing on trivial stuff can be self-serving camouflage. Focusing on the trivial can be a distraction to convince ourselves we are paying attention.

———•———

"Under the tinsel in Hollywood," wrote Ben Hecht, "is more tinsel." Hollywood doesn't just dangle tinsel over our world.

Hollywood is in the tinsel manufacturing business. And we are all buyers.

We long for tinsel in our lives. It makes our dull daily trees seem a little brighter. Stuff is tinsel, and it tinsels our lives. We confuse the stuff of life with stuff because we can buy stuff. But the stuff of life never goes on sale. When we are shopping for the stuff of life, we can't purchase what we haven't earned.

——•—•——

How we look at things is usually influenced by how we see ourselves. When I see myself getting tense and anxious about money and success, I try to hit the brakes. I force myself to remember that as long as I have the wit to dig out a pair of old shorts and running shoes, and the health and will to take a walk on the beach, I'll be okay.

Any of us can be broke and unknown, and the sun can still be on our face, the wind at our back. Next time you're feeling vulnerable, don't go shopping, go walking.

Objects, things, and stuff are often the stuff we hold onto when we feel we have nothing to hold onto. When we're worried we grab for something, and stuff gives us a sense of security. But, "Security," said Helen Keller, "is mostly superstition." We can save stuff but stuff cannot be our savior.

The stuff of faith definitely isn't stuff. A lot of us cling to religious objects when the object of religion is faith. They don't sell ladders to heaven at a hardware store. But we may find our way to heaven by how we treat the clerk at the hardware store. Love is a ladder. It allows us to climb out of ourselves.

A lot of parents will give their kids everything but love, and time, and patience. These gifts never need batteries. Kids never choke on these gifts. Any kid who gets love and time and patience is a rich kid. Any kid who doesn't is poorer for it. And some kids, rich or poor, spend their lives living in the poverty of stuff. Some adults, too.

We spend a lot on stuff but spend the most when we spend our time thinking about stuff. Adding self-insult to self-injury, we spend a lot of time thinking about how we're going to keep our stuff and divide our stuff after we're gone. Even after we lose our bodies we want to make sure our stuff is still around. It's amazing that more of us don't leave a will asking to be stuffed.

Giving people stuff as an expression of love is a habit we carry over into death. Huge fights often occur in families about who's going to get the china that Grandma used, the rocking chair that Grandpa rocked in. Things like this are certainly meaningful to me, but if I don't have them it doesn't mean that Grandma and Grandpa meant any less to me. People we love live in our hearts. And our memories. They are not absent because of their absent human form. They are not gone because they are gone, and they are not here because their stuff is here.

Scientists tell us that our real stuff is our DNA. That this is the stuff of who we are. And yet, Dr. Robert Sapolsky, a professor of biological science and neurology at Stanford University, in a recent *Newsweek* article wrote: "You can't dissociate genes from the environment that turns genes on and off. The more science learns about genes, the more we will learn about the importance of the environment." Even the scientific stuff of life is framed by stuff like caring and attention and support.

It's not all in our genes. Or about how much money we have in our jeans. And certainly not about what pair of designer jeans we're wearing. We tend to forget this because it's easier to open our wallets than to open our hearts. Too many of us think that having more will make us more, as having less makes us less.

Even as many of us are feeling empty inside, our society in the main is overweight. Even as many of us are walking around feeling stuffed, we are craving what stuff can never feed us. Perhaps it's time to stop seeing what more we can grab and pay attention to what is already slipping between our fingers.

———

There is a timeless tale of a poor man who lives in a timeless community. One night, while he sleeps, he dreams. In his dream he is told that there is a treasure cache of gold in a faraway foreign city. The dream directs the dreamer that when he gets to the gates of this city, he will meet a soldier who will lead him to the wealth.

The dream is so real that when the man wakes, he dresses and sets out on a journey to find the treasure. He climbs mountains, fords rivers, crosses plains. He continues on, driven by the dream . . . the dream of wealth.

Eventually he comes to the city in his dreams and, remarkably enough, as foretold, finds a soldier standing at the gates. When he tells his dream to the soldier, the soldier looks astonished. "My friend," he says, "I too had a dream. But if I believed in dreams, I would have climbed mountains, forded rivers, and crossed plains to find the home of a poor man. And there, under his small stove, I would dig and find a treasure."

On hearing this, the man says nothing but turns and sets off toward home. Soon he is again crossing plains, fording rivers, and climbing mountains. Finally, exhausted and at the end of his long efforts, he finds in his small house his large treasure.

———

Life is a treasure, and we spend our lives learning where to dig. Often what we're looking for isn't hidden but, rather, we are blind. Sometimes we look too closely to see what we're really looking at. Occasionally we get the big picture but forget that the details are what make life holy.

———•———

At a local high school graduation, the speaker was a recently retired teacher named Dr. Peter Lorber. As part of his remarks, Dr. Lorber donned the garb of an old prospector and reminded students about what to keep an eye on while, in their lives ahead, they went out looking for gold. "When you get more sand than gold in your pan, and you feel despair, don't forget to look around you," said the teacher in the raspy voice of an old desert rat, "look at the sky and the clouds and the mountains." This man may be retired, but surely he remains a teacher.

Great teachers don't tell us what we see but remind us to open our eyes.

———•———

All of us are prospectors. All of us are looking for gold in our lives. For some of us this gold is gold; for others it is power, fame, a lover, a family, or a friend. Whatever we're looking for, come up empty and you know how a prospector feels.

We've all dug pits looking to uncover what has been buried and have sometimes dug pits for ourselves. What lies buried is often buried within us. The pain and hopes we bury deep inside of us may be the gold we haven't had the courage to mine. We'd all be richer if we stopped picking on others and took a pick to ourselves.

During the summer, when I was kid, endless days were spent playing pickup games of baseball. A group of mixed athletic talent, we would all line up and the two boys at the top of the pecking order would mine the line. In life, some of us look like we're always chosen first, and some of us feel as if we're always chosen last. Sometimes the guys doing the choosing blew it, and like the girl with braces who moved away only to come back a stunning model, the guys forgot to see that the chunky boy from the previous summer was taller, and stronger, and could now belt the ball a mile. Children are a gold mine. Often what they are not is only what neither they nor any one else has YET discovered. Prospectors are people who, instead of minding other people's business, mine their own prospects.

Pyrite is commonly called "fool's gold." Sometimes when we think we've struck it rich, we've only uncovered our foolishness. Fool's gold looks like gold. And has fooled more than a few of us. Who among has not found his or her riches to be fool's gold.

Fool's gold is opaque and brass yellow with a metallic luster and sometimes occurs in association with gold. In life, what's real and what's false don't necessarily live in different neighbor-hoods. Like love and hate, truth and lies, gold and fool's gold are sometimes in proximity.

The vein of gold we're looking for in life is often fed by rivers, and the waters in life are mixed. As is the ore that is pulled from the river of life.

Sometimes in life we feel like we're working in the dark at the bottom of a cave. Occasionally we can light a candle to gain a glimpse, but when we do this we often create as much shadow as light. One of the secrets of success is that success isn't always found in clean, well-lit places. Sometimes to find our inner gold we have to explore the dark side of our soul. Sometimes success requires us to question what our soul considers a success.

Becoming successful sometimes hinges on taking what appears to have less value and making it more. Fool's gold has value, just not the value we have in mind. Pyrite is used mainly in the production of sulfuric acid and ferrous sulfate. Perhaps our own lives would be richer if instead of seeing each other for what we are not, we looked at others for what they might yet become.

What makes pyrite fool's gold is the fool who believes it is gold. Too many of us are fooled because we see others as pyrite instead of as gold.

Prospectors and prophets wander into the desert. Both of them are looking for something. Both of them know that if you're in search of something special, something rare, something that is hidden, sometimes you have to leave the world behind. If we always need to have others around us, we're often missing the company of ourselves. Too many of us confuse the company of fools for gold.

Sometimes to find the inner world you have to leave the outer world. If home is where the heart is, then sometimes we forget that if we're looking for gold we have to look in our homes, in our hearts. Or in the hearts of others.

Love is its own wealth. Ask those without.

Prospectors don't look too neat. They often don't care how they look at all. Too many of us forget what's of value and spend too much time thinking about what we look like or how much others value us.

Each of us is a gold mine. The tragedy of any society is when we lose the value, forget the worth, or waste the resources of the souls in our society. Kids in gangs who are dead by seventeen, moms on welfare for generation after generation, old people forced into retirement and treated with disregard, these are wasted resources and not fool's gold. Our lives are not to be wasted by others or ourselves. Wasting the value of others is not ecologically sound for our society or our soul.

Decades ago, the American inventor and visionary Buckminster Fuller predicted that in the future there will be new mines. "We will," he said, "be mining our garbage dumps." Today that is a big business. We waste much that is precious and have precious little to waste.

A great prospector is someone who knows that you have to weigh your prospects before you weigh your gold. Often in life there is more gold in what we recover than discover. Old romances can hold as much, and sometimes more, treasure than new discoveries. Many of us are prospecting for what we already have.

I was driving down the street the other day and saw a bumper sticker that read, "Resurrection: God's recycling plan." It made me smile. It didn't matter if I agreed with it or not. It made me think. It made me think about how our soul is gold. And like gold, keeps transforming.

You can take gold and make a ring, a coin, or make someone who's poor smile. Be rich in spirit and you can make anything mean more. Be poor in spirit and anything you make doesn't mean much.

There is some new high-tech prospecting going on. Gold is now offshore oil, high-speed chips, turning sand into paper cups. Prospectors, we are discovering, can also be folks with business plans, capital resources, and intentions of going public. But whether you're packing a burro or an aluminum attaché case, whether you make sure to take your canteen or your laptop computer, the one thing you have to take when you go exploring is faith. Across time, faith is the one necessity that every prospector must pack. The irony is that we don't need faith to find gold. We need faith for when we don't. So we don't give up. So we don't forget to look up to see the clouds, and the mountains, and how much we have already been given.

———◆———

A free education isn't free. Mother Teresa used to say, "To keep a lamp burning, we have to keep putting oil in it."

———◆———

Money isn't a dirty word. Like most words, its value is in how you use it.

Use it to light your way and lend a candle to others.

———◆———

20

Personal Improvement

Personal improvement is more than rising to the occasion. Personal improvement is rising from who we are to who we might become.

Rising to who we might yet become is no balloon ride. Rising to these heights takes more than hot air.

Several years ago I had the pleasure of meeting and becoming friends with a wise and kind soul named Ram Dass. Much earlier in his life, Ram Dass had taught at Harvard in the school of psychology under the name Dr. Richard Alpert. Dr. Alpert, along with his now late colleague Dr. Timothy Leary, experimented with many hallucinogenic drugs before turning to a lifelong focus on meditation, reflection, and a profound lifetime of service. One afternoon, as we sat together in the Colorado sunshine, I asked Ram Dass what he now thought about his experience with psychedelics.

White haired and almost bald, my friend ran his hand across the top of his skull and smiled. "What I discovered," he began with a twinkle in his eye, "is that you don't have to get high. You just have to stop doing the things that bring you down."

———•———

Anywhere on this planet, what goes up, comes down. No matter how high you get, sooner or later you're lower. Learning how to get high is often less of a challenge than learning how to land; just as falling in love is very different from landing.

———•———

Ron Morris, who won a silver medal in the pole vault at the Rome Olympics in 1960, smiled not so differently from Ram Dass when I talked to him about the different ways that people could choose to get high in life. "I used to use a metal pole," said Morris, "and then I changed to fiberglass." Like Morris, most of us have changed "poles" in life too. Some who thought drugs would get them high have found that service to others was a higher, more durable high. Some who thought work would get them high in life have found that little gets you higher than love.

What a lot of us have discovered is that work you don't love not only doesn't get you high, it brings you down, while work that fills your heart can be its own lifelong partner.

Few of us are among the best pole-vaulters in the world. All of us are learning how to fall and land. And where to find the strength to get up again.

It's worth noting that it was only in the twentieth century that we as human beings escaped the gravitational bonds of earth. Before recently there were no airplanes, jets, rockets, or spaceships. There were, of course, hot air balloons, but across time more of us were filled with hot air than were getting higher.

Needless to say, the most neurotic path to personal improvement is by attempting to bring others down.

Telling others who are different what they can't do is the way some folks think they're making a difference.

Some people aren't going to be happy until you're as unhappy as they are.

——•—•——

The rush to remind others of what they don't know, who they will never become, why they can't achieve is the worst way to gain altitude.

Clipping other people's wings doesn't help us fly.

Putting a hole in someone else's balloon doesn't fill ours.

——•—•——

The urge to gain height and sail away is as primal as the need to be connected and grounded.

——•—•——

Early in the development of flight, the Wright brothers had to go abroad in order to secure proper recognition for their aeronautic achievements. The French government welcomed them and gave the brothers an opportunity to demonstrate what they had done; but as a group, the French showed more of their jealousy to the two Yanks.

Following the successful proof by the Wright brothers, a banquet in Paris was arranged in their honor. At the dinner, there was a great deal of speech-making. The chief orator was a distinguished Frenchman who devoted most of his remarks to claiming that France had led the world in the new field of endeavor and would do so in the future. The speaker had very little to say in praise of the two chief guests.

When Wilbur Wright was called upon to speak, he rose slowly to his feet. "I am no hand at public speaking," said Wright, "and on this occasion must content myself with a few words. As I sat here listening to the speaker who preceded me I have heard comparisons made to the eagle, to the swallow, and to the hawk as typifying skill and speed in the mastery of the air; but, some-how or other, I could not keep from thinking of the parrot which, of all the ornithological kingdom, is the poorest flier and the best talker."

No matter how high a parrot flies it remains a parrot.

———•·•———

Some of us never fly but spend our lives in the control tower telling others when to land and where to land.

Some of us with little experience in aeronautical mechanics spend more time trying to clip the wings of others than working on our own wings.

Any of us who want to be highfliers need to know what every great pilot has learned. The heavens are inaccessible to those who haven't done their work on earth.

———•·•———

The golfer Arnold Palmer once said, "It's a funny thing, the more I practice the luckier I get."

In learning and love, in work and war, inches and quarter inches matter. Bullets that miss the heart by inches, or hurts that inch toward the heart, make this point.

Few of us will reach the stars but all of us can aim a little higher. Even if it's inches higher. "Help someone up their mountain," said an anonymous sage, "and you can't help but get a little closer to the top yourself."

Personal improvement happens only to people who are becoming better persons.

The Wright brothers had it right. How high we get in life has less to do with what we say and more to do with what we do. We don't have to get high. We just have to stop doing the things that are bringing us down.

"It matters not what you are thought to be, but what you are," said Publilius Syrus. Don't let your thoughts limit your thinking. Don't let who you think you are limit who you are.

It isn't as if we get up in the morning and put on a mask. It is rather that too many of us go to bed wearing a mask and wake the same way. We not only mask our face, we also mask our ambition and our expectations. Personal improvement requires us to unmask our potential, even if it is only to ourselves.

Even those of us who don't wear makeup often make up how we want to be seen. Too many of us who want to be seen a certain way are coming apart at the seams. "The challenge in life," said the early twentieth-century philosopher Martin Buber, "is to move from seeming to being."

Be who you are and let others worry about who you seem to be.

No matter what age we are, no matter if we're in school, or in the school of hard knocks, why not think about an interior graduation? Why not think about graduating from seeming to being?

———

Sometimes what we refuse to see shows us how we were raised to see.

———

Moving from seeming to being isn't something you do for others. It's something everyone has to do for themselves.

Wanting to be thought of as considerate is sometimes our mask for not wanting to risk disapproval. The source of much dishonesty, to self and others, isn't a fear that others will hurt us, but that they won't love us.

We all want to be loved, or at least appreciated. We all need public and intimate affirmation. We all need affirmation from others and a significant other. All the world may be a stage, but all of us need applause from both the exterior and interior audience. Sometimes no crowd boos louder than the single voice inside our soul. Or applauds louder.

I had dinner one evening with a man of God. His name is Father Virgil. He is a man who has said that "truth is humility" and conducts himself with both humility and truth. In the course of our conversation, he shared an idea that continues to resonate. "Much of our struggle," said Father Virgil, "is to accept God's acceptance of us."

Before we can be accepting of others, we must learn to accept who we are. The whole cast of who we are. If there are parts we play that we don't like, we can work on them but not by denying them. Before we go onto the social stage, perhaps we need to look at all the characters in our company and see ourselves as the hero and villain, divine and deception, delight and despair.

Shakespeare wrote: "Life is a tale told by an idiot, full of sound and fury signifying nothing." The Bard was wise and now and then wrong. Excuse the double negative, but even our nothingness is not nothing. The parts of us that are missing, the parts we have not become, yet, the silent parts of ourselves are part of the composition. It is the silence between the notes that makes the music.

Likewise, it is the space between the bars that holds the tiger. Our fears hold our fears. And it takes strength to know this.

———•◆•———

To move from seeming to being with others requires, as Father Virgil reminds us, the strength to accept that we are accepted. We are the tiger striking fear in our own heart. The roar in our lives late at night is often the roar of that part of us that wants to be let out of the socially correct cage, or our socially correct doubts of our potential, where we have penned ourselves. In the lion's den, we are Daniel and the lion.

All confession is first to ourselves.

————

The need to talk with God is a way God affords us to talk with ourselves.

The real question isn't if God's listening, but if we are. To ourselves.

Atheists, agnostics, and true believers all share one belief. People of every faith and no faith all believe they have the right to be insincere to themselves.

Dr. Phillip Eisenberg, in his book from 1946 titled *Why We Act the Way We Do,* writes,

"We often hide our true feelings from ourselves, sometimes by acting out their opposite cleverly enough to fool even ourselves. A man may disguise a desire for power as altruism. Because he does not want to admit that he wants power, he seeks a more acceptable form of obtaining it. By helping others, he gains the feeling that others need him and that he is a superior person."

————

Personal improvement means working to graduate from good to better, from better to better yet. This is not something we attain, but spend a lifetime working toward. All art is failure because it falls just short of the truth. The finest painting of a rose is not a rose. We are not failures if we are not who we might become. We are failures if we do not make the attempt.

We are all becoming who we are, and so to be true to ourselves means to approach a target that is constantly moving.

Choose your target carefully. What's important is that we are moving toward being who we are instead of always trying to be who we thought others thought we should be.

Personal improvement isn't necessarily about moving on to a strange new world but moving closer to your strange new self. Becoming who you are.

To all of you who are in school or in the graduate school of life experiences, welcome to the wonderful world of becoming you. To all of us who are out of school, write yourself a hall pass to leave a life of seeming and get permission to be who you are. To all of us who are in process, be of good cheer. You are not alone.

———•◦•———

"Against every great and noble endeavor," said Einstein, "are a thousand mediocre minds." If you're looking for appreciation in your efforts at personal improvement, look in the dictionary. All real growth is private, at least at first.

Jean-Dominique Bauby died recently in Paris. He was 44. He was a journalist who had a stroke, woke paralyzed, and wrote a widely praised novel by blinking, 200,000 times. "Bauby's book," said the Associated Press, "is gripping, never maudlin. There's frustration when a fly sits stubbornly on his nose, or when an aide switches off a soccer match during halftime, blind to his furiously batting eyelid. There's bemused annoyance when an orderly wishes him 'bon appétit' before meals containing brown gook moving through a tube to his stomach. There's heartbreak when he can't hold his children."

———•◦•———

Too many of us walk around feeling sorry for ourselves when we would be better served to be inspired by those who legitimately could walk their despair and don't. Too many of us, for lack of something we want to watch on television, cast ourselves in our own soap operas. Too many of us want the world to say, "I'm sorry," as opposed to asking ourselves, "What's our excuse?"

Reading the story about Mr. Bauby, I experience a recovery from my self-imposed restraints. My little aches and pains, my petty complaints of the day, my imagined fears about fortune and fame were, as the television evangelist puts it in three syllables: He-al-ed!

Reading the story about Mr. Bauby, I knew I had to cancel my plans. I had to call back the invitations to my pity-party. Mr. Bauby's heroism had ruined a good feeling-sorry-for-myself that my emotions had just RSVP'd.

Too many of us use self-pity to define self.

What matters is what we do, not why we didn't.

There are dark days and dark figures in all of our dramas. Some of us are married to life for better and some for worse. Life's triumph is not the grand excuse, but how we act when we have every right to an excuse.

Personal improvement begins with what we get up and do. And don't do.

What we do when we can't do anymore makes us more.
Things don't have to be good for us to be great.

There are philosophies that tell us that life is an experience
viewed through a veil of tears. This perception, however, is not
my idea of admiring a waterfall. Eeyore is the character in
Winnie the Pooh who always acquires an attitude before he acts.
He moans before he moves. Too many of us whine about life's
wine. Drink up. The wine is always better than the whine.
Sometimes wine just needs to breathe a little. In life, much is
gained simply by taking a deep breath.

"Courage," says an old American proverb, "is fear that has said
its prayers." We all feel a little weak-kneed at the prospect of
moving into unknown terrain or through known fears. But
prayer is a path where there is none, wisdom is a compass, and
hope is a lantern.

Sure there are mosquitoes, and on everyone's expedition you
have to swat a few. On life's journey, creepy things, big and
small, seldom stay behind screen doors.

"It is also art," said Thoreau, "to make the day beautiful." We are
a canvas of opportunity. How we portray the world we see
makes our life art and art life.

Life is not painting by the numbers. Life is learning to trust that
we can make something beautiful when we decide to paint
bright yellow where the number "13" directs us to paint black.
Excuse me. None of us are copies. All of us are original art
of the Master Artist. God's signature is our soul. And we are
therefore infinite and infinite in our capacity.

Others have the right to be excused from our expectations, but all of us should expect great things of ourselves.

Tolstoy's work would have been lost to the world had his wife not stayed up nights rewriting by hand, letter by letter, his impenetrable script. One can't help but wonder how much of Tolstoy is Mrs. Tolstoy.

Keep an eye on being great rather than worrying about being in the public eye.

———————

A friend of mine from South Africa told me that his mother, Sara, used to say, "Be happy with your little in life and you'll be happy with your lot."

A lot of us could benefit from remembering that. Even those who have a little can discover that it means a lot. Too many of us who have a lot are still caught in the wake of wanting a little more. Some a lot more.

———————

History is often not what we did but what we choose to remember doing. And the future what we choose to do.

We often don't look behind us to see those who by our wake we've knocked off their surfboards, tumbled their sailboats, collapsed their docks. So often in life we are just out there with our boilers filled to bursting, all of our canvas catching wind, our cannons firing salvo after salvo chasing pirates, the fair princess, or distant treasure. Watch the water ahead of you. Mind your wake.

There is romance in knowing we are a ship at sea. There is adventure in thinking of ports we have never seen. What's worth remembering is that every moment is a port we have never before visited. What port in your potential do you yet want to visit?

There is an old saying: "Every time history repeats itself the price goes up." The significance of what has happened is enhanced by what we make of it or make happen. Or ignore.

——•—•——

My mother is almost eighty and infirm. Her husband is older yet. The two of them are leaving this morning on a five-day cruise. "I'm determined to go while I still can," says my mother when she tells me her plans. In her determination I hear her heroism for living. I call them to say good-bye. "I've got my doubts," says her husband. "Leave your doubts at home and pack your hope," I say. "I hope so," he says. "Bon voyage," I tell my mother, and suddenly hear in my words a metaphor to mortality. "I just mean have a great trip," I say. "I know," she says. But she knows. And I know. And none of us know when our cruise will get caught in the wake of God's intentions. Weigh anchor, life is short. Shout "ahoy" to someone you love, or something you would still love to do, or to someone you would still love to be.

——•—•——

Whether we're rowboats or aircraft carriers, whether we're dinghies or feeling dingy or doing great, all of us are riding out our lives. We all live in the wake of great ships. Being great sometimes means nothing more than staying afloat.

——•—•——

"A rising tide," says an ancient Asian wisdom, "lifts all boats."

May you be lifted.

May you lift others.

May you not only rise occasionally in life, but to the occasion of living.

———

As our planet evolved, the weather changed, and life on our planet evolved along with the weather. Survival was intimately linked to evolution. And still is. To beat extinction here are a few rules that I have picked up from a lifelong interest in dinosaurs:

1. Don't take a Jacuzzi in a tar pit.

2. When you hit forty tons, stop eating.

3. Don't eat your young.

4. Stay indoors during an ice age.

5. Remember, what isn't adapting, is dying.

———

Dinosaurs were around for about 200 million years but recorded history is only 10,000 years, and if we, as human beings, want to make it for even a fraction of that time, we might want to take note of what happened to the "big ones" and take some notes.

One of the early and largest dinosaurs was the Diplodocus. It was a forerunner of the Brontosaurus. This was a huge herbivore with a long neck that allowed it to eat at the tops of trees. It ate two tons a day and left a ton of feces every day. Here's a lesson. The more we consume, the more we leave behind. Sometimes we can find who among us has the biggest appetite by how much they leave in their wake. Any of us who think we are really "big-timers" might stop to look at what we leave behind us, ask ourselves how we can be sure others aren't stepping in it, and who's supposed to clean it up? Just as we're told to clean up after our pet, we might want to do the same for our ego. Talk about lugging a baggie for a walk in the park.

The Diplodocus had a tail about as long as its neck. This was the way the dinosaur kept its balance. And kept itself alive. The neck allowed it to eat. The tail could swat at enemies. Little serves any of us more than finding our balance. If we don't balance what we reach for with what we can grab, it will cause us to fall. "Man over-leaps himself," wrote Shakespeare. It doesn't matter how big you are. If you lose your balance, you're history. Ask the Diplodocus.

Dinosaurs that were huge made a huge target. Large predators like larger prey. Paint yourself self-important and you're painting a bull's eye on your behind. Social and business predators aren't going to miss a meal the size of a buffet table. Self-importance makes us easy pickings and is a neon sign telling others to put on a bib.

There's always a bigger fish, and everybody is always on somebody's menu.

Scientists remind us the demise of dinosaurs wasn't finally from any natural enemies. What we're naturally inclined to worry about isn't necessarily the nature of our problems. What we worry most about in life is often not what we should be worrying about. A fair number of mastodons did wind up on the saber tooth tiger's dinner menu, but a meteor and swamps and ice and drought did the major dirty work. Any of us who think we're king of the hill may think that we can relax after a day of stomping through the jungle, but we'd be well advised to watch which tar pit we use as a hot tub.

"More of us die from overeating," wrote Rabbi Nachman of Bratslav two hundred years ago, "than die from undernourishment." Certainly in this day and time, good times kill as many of us as hard times.

A psychiatrist friend recently reminded me few of us can bear the burden of uncertainty. Consequently it is in our nature to either act on our uncertainty or to deny it. For dinosaurs, ironically, and for many of us almost certainly, the question is the reverse. How can we survive our own strengths? How can we keep from suffocating under our greatest attributes? This remains worth thinking about right now, before time walks around in our remains.

Time is a tar pit. Every moment is trapped in time. But not necessarily victimized. "The basis for wisdom," wrote the philosopher Spinoza, "is not in the reflection on death, but in the reflection on life." Paying attention to what is extinct may keep us from becoming extinct. Paying attention to the life we may yet have a chance to live is the way to develop and live.

What's normal is that there is no norm. Oh, we may have thought there was a norm a few years ago. Or a hundred years ago. But the river looks like it's running straight only when you're standing right next to the shore. Pull back a bit, step back a few years, get some distance on anyone or anything we know or knew, and we discover that everything and everyone has their bends, their twists. And that's normal.

———

The world has never held still. The world is an object in orbit, in its spin, but isn't spinning out of control.

It is only our urge to control the world, or the naïve notion that we can stand still and look at the world, that makes things appear out of control. In reality it's our perception that's out of control. We are on a spinning ball observing a spinning universe. That's it. Oh, what a spin we're all in and personal improvement is not something that can wait for the world to slow down. Won't happen. Can't happen.

Stability isn't the absence of storms in one's life but finding the quiet at the center of the storm.

———

Winds of change haven't just started blowing. Change is the river we all sail on.

And always have sailed on.

———

Today is another day, and the stuff we didn't do still needs to get done or be left undone and leave us feeling undone.

If there was ever a season of new beginnings, this is it because the world is turning and every day is a new season. And today is a perfect season to begin being more than we were last season.

The only way to begin these days is to begin. Begin without expectation. Begin here. Begin now. Show up.

———•—•———

Little digs us out of problems in life like digging in.

"I'll have a new day," sang the poet Jim Croce, "if she'll have me." Ask the moment to marry you because you're wed to it— for the moment.

———•—•———

And yes, we should think about what we're getting into at any moment, but thinking about what will happen might not do as much good as we might think. Much of what we're thinking about is no longer what it was, and the way we're used to thinking often isn't the way things are any longer working. More and more often we have to play life like a golf game—play it as it lays.

I don't play golf, but as I understand the game, even when we've taken a bad swing at things we can't kick the ball back to where it was five thousand years or five minutes ago. Play life as it lays. Play through. Get on with your life. And don't forget to sight the flag. If you want to sink the shot.

The first words in the Bible are: "In the beginning . . ." It does not begin with, "at the beginning." Every beginning is part of a process. What we choose to call "the beginning" in anything is a point in a process that we have stop-framed so we can see what's happening in an event that won't sit still. Life doesn't listen when the photographer tells a wiggling moment, "You have to sit still."

———•—•———

Hockey-great Wayne Gretzky was schooled early in the game by his father. "You can teach anticipation," said Walter Gretzky, explaining Wayne's uncanny ability to know not only where the puck is but where it would be.

——•◦•——

With practice we can know what we're supposed to say in almost any old script. But in that script we knew how the play turned out. Trust me, in the today-play no one knows how the play turns out—whether it's a comedy or a tragedy—or how many acts there will be. Knowing what we will say on stage works only when we know what has already been said.

The best way to get a new part in life's play is to stop rehearsing the past.

"We do not know whether the things afflicting us," said the South American author Jorge Luis Borges, "are the secret beginning of our happiness or not."

Being where we are is the best way to get where we're going.

"Like all great travelers," said Benjamin Disraeli, "I have seen more than I remember, and remember more than I have seen."

——•◦•——

We are all travelers.

May you go from strength to strength and be a source of strength for others.

——•◦•——

A Note From the Editor

Dear Reader,

I have been fortunate enough to not only work with Noah benShea directly, but also to hear him speak before audiences of academics, employees, and educators. He is truly compelling, and upon hearing him speak I have often found my thoughts struggling to keep up with his words. Not that his delivery was ponderous, mind you, but rather I found myself pondering over certain passages, weighing their relevance to my life and the lives of those around me, and enjoying his ability to make me think deeply and appreciatively. He has a fundamental ability to turn common phrases into more provoking reflections that do indeed inspire, motivate, and enlighten us.

There is great personal joy in having Noah's work in print, available for me to linger over at my own leisure. His thoughts travel well, and travel with me. Yet nothing can equate with that visceral reaction to his public speaking, the unique physical and cognitive response that one has as the speech unfolds around and beneath and above you.

My letter to you closes this new book from Noah, yet I encourage you to continue to seek him out. Go hear and feel him speak if you have the opportunity. Perhaps bring him into your own community or school. It is truly a moving experience that will remain with you. And as others have done and continue to do, write to him with your questions or thoughts. Ask for his take on your issues. He is unusually accessible and interested, and far more often than not will help you see things from another, often more copasetic perspective. He is as close as noah@noahswindow.com.

Sincerely,

Robert D. Clouse

CORWIN PRESS

The Corwin Press logo—a raven striding across an open book—represents the happy union of courage and learning. We are a professional-level publisher of books and journals for K-12 educators, and we are committed to creating and providing resources that embody these qualities. Corwin's motto is "Success for All Learners."